BROKEN CHAINS

A POETIC JOURNEY FROM TRAGEDY TO GLORY

LAKITA PATTON

BROKEN CHAINS

A POETIC JOURNEY FROM TRAGEDY TO GLORY

LAKITA PATTON

Detroit, MI, USA

Broken Chains: A Poetic Journey from Tragedy to Glory
Copyright © 2016 Lakita Patton

All scripture quotations, unless otherwise indicated, are taken from the HOLY BIBLE, KING JAMES VERSION.

Scripture quotations taken from the New American Standard Bible®, Copyright © 1960, 1962, 1963, 1968, 1971, 1972, 1973, 1975, 1977, 1995 by The Lockman Foundation. Used by permission." (www.Lockman.org) and are marked (NASB).

All rights reserved. No part of this publication may be reproduced, stored in a retrieval system, or transmitted in any form or by any means – electronic, mechanical, photocopy, recording, or any other – except for brief quotations in printed reviews, without the prior permission of the publisher.

NOTE:

The author acknowledges that all references to the God of the Bible and His Divine attributes are capitalized to honor His majesty.

*Priority*ONE Publications
P. O. Box 34722 • Detroit, MI 48234 USA
E-mail: info@priorityonebooks.com
URL: http://www.priorityonebooks.com

ISBN 13:   978-1-933972-48-0
ISBN 10:   1-933972-48-3

Editing by PriorityONE Publications
Front cover design by Moises DeJesus for Chedda International®
Back cover and interior design by PriorityONE Publications

Printed in the United States of America

CONTENTS

LēTTI NG Gō 9
    THE INTRODUCTION 11
    STOP HALF-STEPPING
    I'M NOT HALF-STEPPING ON YOU 14
    PRESSURE BRINGS FORTH PRAISE 17
    "OUT OF THEM ALL" 19
    REGAIN STRENGTH 21
    THE STORMS OF RAGING CHAOS 24
    LET GO 27
    SEPARATIONS BRING PERMEATIONS 29
    STAY FOCUSED 32
    THE BIGGEST LIE OF SATAN 35
    THE BREATH OF MISERY 38
    THE RIVERS OF PAIN 40
    PURGED 42
    LORD HELP ME 44
    THE HURRICANE SYNDROME 46
    THE SHACKELS THAT PULL ME DOWN 49
    RELEASE 51
    MOUNTAINS 53
    JUST LET GO 55
    PERSONAL REFLECTIONS 56

ē NDURING 59
    INTRODUCTION 61
    POWER 66

PERSEVERE YOUR DESTINY IS NEAR	68
THE HELMET	70
AS I AM	73
THE RED SEA	76
YOU CANNOT FOOL ME	78
90 DAYS IN A DISASTER	80
COLLISION	82
ACCOMPLISHMENTS	84
THE DESTINY THAT CAPTURED ME	86
THE DEATH OF MISERY	88
WHY?	90
YOU FORGOT YOUR ASSIGNMENT	92
THE SUDDEN SHORE	94
CAN YOU DISTINGUISH THE TWO? WHO IS REALLY SPEAKING THROUGH YOU?	96
LONGSUFFERING	101
PERSONAL REFLECTIONS	102
Nē WNē SS	**105**
INTRODUCTION	107
THE NEW YOU	109
THE SILENT WHISPER	112
AS THE WIND BLOWS	114
NEWNESS AWAITS YOU	116
RELATIONSHIP VS RELIGION	118
YOU MAY HAVE FELL BUT HIS LOVE PREVAILS	120
I HAVE A NEW NAME	123
LOOK UP	125
PRESS IN	128

CLEAN HOUSE ... 130
TAKE UP THY BED IN WALK ... 132
OUR GOD ... 134
FOLLOW THE PRINCIPLES AND NOT THE PLEASURE ... 136
PERSONAL REFLECTIONS ... 138

Rē STō RATIō N ... 141
INTRODUCTION ... 143
THE LAMP STAND ... 147
BIRTHING ... 149
THERE IS HEALING IN REVEALING ... 151
FREE ... 153
SALVATION ... 155
CALL IT OUT ... 158
REST IN THE TEST ... 161
FEAR NOT. COME ALIVE ... 163
DIG DEEPER ... 165
WAR ... 167
AWAKEN IN YOUR SPIRIT ... 169
THE LOVE THAT STOLE MY HEART ... 172
OVERCOMING ... 174
NO MORE WHIRLWINDS ... 176
GOD WANTS YOU ... 178
SELF CONTROL ... 180
OVERSEER ... 182
I AM CHANGED ... 184
WE WON'T BE AFRAID ... 187
I'M STICKING WITH JESUS ... 189
JESUS IS THE WAY ... 192

THE VINE 194
PERSONAL REFLECTIONS 195
ABōUT LAKITA PATTōN 197

LETTING GO

THE INTRODUCTION

The freedom of letting go of pains, hurts, and un-forgiveness is so refreshing. It lifts the burdens from your soul so that you are able to live without allowing the weight of past mistakes make you think it's too late. I grew up in a very dysfunctional family where there was no love. I remember when I was only four, my mom, my two sisters, and I lived in an apartment building. Because the apartment building was very old we had to move out of suddenly, after having stayed there for a while. That week we had to pack up as we prepared to live with our grandmother, who stayed right behind us. As a child, I slept very hard. I literally had to be shaken so that I could wake up. That morning, I was awakened with a gentle touch – today I know it was the Holy Spirit. To this day He awakens me gently. I realized that I was left alone in the building. I began to cry as I searched the apartment calling for my sisters and mom, but no one was there. Our apartment had a pantry that my sisters and I would play in from time to time, so my hopes were that I would eventually find them there, but it was not so. I had a friend which was a teddy bear, I could not even find him either. I remember feeling afraid because of the fact I was alone in this building. I remembered that my mom told us that the building we lived in would have to be demolished. I cried so hard searching that small apartment and all my loved ones did not answer. I eventually went to the apartment down stairs to my mom's close friend, who cared for us like an aunt, but no one was there either. As I called to her three daughters, which were very close to my sisters and me, still no answer.

Finally, that same gentle touch directed me outside. When I went outside there was a man in the garage and when he looked at me, I felt as though he would kill and rape me. Later on that day, I overheard my mother, sister, and grandmother saying that he was a drug addict, trying to find something to sell. I walked as fast as I could through the field to my grandmother's house, and I found my sisters and mom there.

My aunt and mom told me shut up and asked, "Why are you crying?" That question left me so confused, so I asked, "Why did you leave me by myself?" I got a whipping then told I was wrong for asking that question. My aunt said, "You were sleep! Nothing was gonna happen to you, girl. Now sit your fat self down!" Then she yanked my arm pulling me down to the floor next to her as she sat in the chair. Those moments left me terrified. Anytime I would sleep at night I was afraid that if I awakened I wouldn't find my sisters and mom. That was how I began operating from a mindset of abandonment. Walking into my grandmother house that day was the beginning of a tragic childhood.

The poems in this book describe the emotional and mental suffering I endured as I tried to find peace, in the chaotic world that had me bound. Surrendering my raw pain to God helped me to walk with Him as He taught me that He really loved me. He not only wanted to help me, He had the power to set me free.

Sometimes people can't find the words to fully describe the torment their dysfunctional families caused them, or the foolish choices they made as a result. But, they want and need to be free. My hope is that within these poems, others will find the words necessary to acknowledge and work through the hurt, shame, anger, and frustration they feel. Then prayerfully, like me, they can truly find the kind of love, joy, and peace that never fades, because God has broken their chains.

*"Do not give what is holy to dogs,
and do not throw your pearls before swine,
or they will trample them under their feet,
and turn and tear you to pieces.
Ask, and it will be given to you; seek,
and you will find; knock, and it will be opened to you."*
Matthew 7:6-7 NASB

STOP HALF-STEPPING
I'M NOT HALF-STEPPING ON YOU

You want me to do what you want, and at the same time,
you are not doing what I say.
Stop half-stepping. I am not half-stepping on you.

I am always present but when I call, where are you?
Stop half- stepping. I am not half-stepping on you.

You make these bold long suggestions but when I supply,
you rebuke my blessing.
Stop half-stepping. I am not half-stepping on you.

In the midst of all your pain you called for me I came to see;
yielded, then sent you help.
It was not at your convenience, so you turned your cheek,
and waved your hand.
Stop half-stepping I am not half-stepping on you.

Activate James 2:14-26, then you will not be so belligerent.
Stop half-stepping I will not and cannot half-step on you.

The earth, I've given that to you,
but you won't trust in my eyes to see you through.
So just stop half-stepping surely I am not half-stepping on you.

That pain, I know it is a burden.
Give it to me, I will carry it for you.
Just stop half-stepping because I am not half-stepping on you.

That corruption, you won't even pray to me and yet you say I am angry?
Stop half-stepping. I promise I am not half-stepping on you.

I am always here. It's you that disappears.
Stop half-stepping I am not half stepping on you.

God is teaching us to fight in the power of His might.
God is instructing us on how to rise above obstacles through His Word.

Therefore, you can rise in the beauty of the Holy Spirit.
Stop half-stepping. He is not half-stepping on you.

Seek Him in all that you say and do.
Stop half-stepping. He is not half stepping on you.

In order to prosper you have to transition from religion to relationship.
You must deny your own occupations to receive Christ's destinations.
Stop half-stepping. He is not half-stepping on you.

Your opinions have nothing to do with Christ's dominions.
Stop half-stepping. God told you, "I am not half-stepping on you!"

Just because you are in the storms of raging chaos,
His grace is never ending nonstop.
Stop half-stepping God is not half-stepping on you.

There is greatness right the inside of you,
so stop playing Russian roulette and let His hands guide you.
Then God shall supply. He doesn't lie.
It is time to believe beyond extreme.
Stop half-stepping because He is not half-stepping on you.

¹Arise, shine; for thy light is come,
and the glory of the L{\small ORD} *is risen upon thee.*
²For, behold, the darkness shall cover the earth,
and gross darkness the people:
but the L{\small ORD} *shall arise upon thee,*
and his glory shall be seen upon thee.

Isaiah 60:1-2

The Spirit of the Lord God is upon me;
because the Lord hath anointed me to preach good tidings unto the meek;
he hath sent me to bind up the brokenhearted,
to proclaim liberty to the captives,
and the opening of the prison to them that are bound;

Isaiah 60:1

PRESSURE BRINGS FORTH PRAISE

Pressure brings forth praise, if you allow it to.
The Master Physician has done surgery on you.
Those corrupt seeds have to come out of you.
It's causing your baby to not push through.

You know that you are pregnant.
It is evident because of what God has placed within you.
Pressure brings forth praise if allow it to.
Nothing can stop you but praise shall get you through.

Because greater is that on the inside you!
Protect your mind at all times; the Holy Spirit is just like a vacuum
He sucks up all impurity, while establishing unity.
Pressure brings forth praise if you allow it to.

Place your foot on that solid ground and drink from the fountain of life.
Set your mind totally on Christ. Even in the midst of hardships.
Pressure brings forth praise if you allow it to.

Those labor pains will almost drive you insane.
Just look up and praise His great name.
You do not need manmade medications for those pains
when all you have to do is sing, holy, holy is Your great name.
Pressure brings forth praise if you allow it to.

So what if people look at you and expect something different.
While you are under pressure go forth in power also aggression. Sever the umbilical cord of depression that is connected to oppression.
Silence the thought of neglect and stressing throughout each trimester reap the benefits from blessing.
Pressure brings forth praise if you allow it to.

What shall you fear? Your destiny is near!
Pressure brings forth praise.
So praise while pushing through.

¹I will bless the Lord at all times:
his praise shall continually be in my mouth.
²My soul shall make her boast in the Lord
the humble shall hear thereof, and be glad.
³O magnify the Lord with me, and let us exalt his name together.
⁴I sought the Lord, and he heard me, and delivered me from all my fears.
⁵They looked unto him, and were lightened:
and their faces were not ashamed.
⁶This poor man cried, and the Lord heard him,
and saved him out of all his troubles.
⁷The angel of the Lord encampeth round about them that fear him,
and delivereth them.
⁸O taste and see that the Lord is good:
blessed is the man that trusteth in him.
⁹O fear the Lord, ye his saints: for there is no want to them that fear him.
¹⁰The young lions do lack, and suffer hunger:
but they that seek the Lord shall not want any good thing.
¹¹Come, ye children, hearken unto me:
I will teach you the fear of the Lord.
¹²What man is he that desireth life,
and loveth many days, that he may see good?
¹³Keep thy tongue from evil, and thy lips from speaking guile.
¹⁴Depart from evil, and do good; seek peace, and pursue it.
¹⁵The eyes of the Lord are upon the righteous,
and his ears are open unto their cry.
¹⁶The face of the Lord is against them that do evil,
to cut off the remembrance of them from the earth.
¹⁷The righteous cry, and the Lord heareth,
and delivereth them out of all their troubles.
¹⁸The Lord is nigh unto them that are of a broken heart;
and saveth such as be of a contrite spirit.
¹⁹Many are the afflictions of the righteous:
but the Lord delivereth him out of them all.
²⁰He keepeth all his bones: not one of them is broken.
²¹Evil shall slay the wicked:
and they that hate the righteous shall be desolate.
²²The Lord redeemeth the soul of his servants:
and none of them that trust in him shall be desolate.

Psalm 34

"OUT OF THEM ALL"

Persecutions are a part of the believer's walk with Christ.
Learn how to trust God in all of your problems,
no matter what they are.

Preparation is the main key to success with the best.
Out of them all giants must fall.

Sometimes you have to keep what the Holy Spirit has given you.
A secret you must learn;
be as faithful to JESUS as He is faithful to you, at all times.

Most people won't understand
that despite all you have gone through you're still able
to move towards the promise land.

Being uncomfortable is okay.
It means you depend on God
as He leads the way.

Glory be to God in the highest!
As you move and activate your faith
you will hear the enemy screaming, "It's too late."

Lift up the name of JESUS anyway.
You're going to feel weary,
but out of them all His peace surpasses all understanding.

Are you going to serve the Creator of the world with gladness,
or serve the serpent with groaning?
If you know that His presence never forsakes you,
then mount up, stand tall, surrender your brokenness as He restores.

You shall shimmer with beauty
wrapped in His strong and mighty arms,
never giving up, knowing by faith that through all of this,
He delivered me OUT OF THEM ALL.

*[10] Finally, my brethren, be strong in the Lord,
and in the power of his might.
[11] Put on the whole armour of God,
that ye may be able to stand against the wiles of the devil.
[12] For we wrestle not against flesh and blood,
but against principalities, against powers,
against the rulers of the darkness of this world,
against spiritual wickedness in high places.
[13] Wherefore take unto you the whole armour of God,
that ye may be able to withstand in the evil day,
and having done all, to stand.
[14] Stand therefore, having your loins girt about with truth,
and having on the breastplate of righteousness;
[15] And your feet shod with the preparation of the gospel of peace;
[16] Above all, taking the shield of faith,
wherewith ye shall be able to quench all the fiery darts of the wicked.
[17] And take of salvation,
and the sword of the Spirit, which is the word of God:*

Ephesians 6:10-17

REGAIN STRENGTH

Faith is a positive action;
negativity is a distraction for an ungodly reaction.
What is against you cannot defeat you.
God did not draw you out of the pit to go back into foolishness.
You just forgot to regain your strength.

There is no need to keep drawing back
when the power is rooted in your thinking.
You just have to regain your strength.

Fear corrupts your soul and you're created to be bold.
You just have to regain your strength.

There are things we will never understand.
Move from that dry place, learn the character of Jesus
and do not lose concentration. Regain strength.

Being alone in the wilderness, do not worry. It's okay.
You must gain the power to complete the tasks.
This too shall pass.

Look to the hills and learn devotions,
also rebuke broken emotions. Do not be bound.
Regain your strength.

If you do not speak up, you are choked up
living a lie just to get by deceptions caused by rejection.
Satan wants to control while manipulating you.
Submit to the King and he will flee from you. Regain your strength.

It's never about what you want to do.
But it's about what has been laid up for you.
Regain strength.

God's desire is that you do things with excellence,
while reaping heavenly benefits.
Your obedience is connected to how much you love Him.
So refuse to place anything above Him. Regain strength.

Wait on God as He decontaminates the land.
He has to perform a spiritual cleansing.
There was too much darkness and a whole lot of clutter,
generational cursers from your mother.
Regain strength.

Discipline your mouth and what you speak,
the rivers of life have to flow from you.
Regain strength.

A fool hates correction, do not complain.
Just remain humble.
Regain your strength.

You have been down too long, do not lose hope.
Regaining strength has its benefits.

When others are weeping from giving birth prematurely, you're rejoicing.
When others are down trodden, you are smiling.
When others have lost their way,
God will see fit to call on you to see them through.
Regain strength.

While others have died because pride has crept inside,
the light of CHRIST will shine bright through you.
Regain your strength.

You will not sit here and die.
There are nations attached to you.
Regain strength.

Even when all hell comes against you, regain strength.
Christ is hope for the hopeless and food for the hungry,
shelter for the poor, eyes for the blind, and cure for sickness.
REGAIN YOUR STRENGH.

Thou hypocrite, first cast out the beam out of thine own eye; and then shalt thou see clearly to cast out the mote out of thy brother's eye.

Matthew 7:5

THE STORMS OF RAGING CHAOS

There has to be something that makes this storms stop.
So many clouds and they are forming raging chaos.

I try to get away from all this mess,
but the more I move to a safe haven,
the same old storms come rushing in.

I'm looking around at war wondering,
"How did this raging chaos get in?"
I have not even desired to look at me;
I feel that mirror cannot maintain me.

So I blame everyone else,
not realizing this storm of raging chaos was created by me.
I have no motives to change.
I'm used to shame.

Raging in anger because I was abused by a stranger,
I just want to crawl up and die,
because my foundation was built on lies.
I might as well commit suicide.

I try to make peace.
But as soon as I open my mouth to speak,
the storms of a raging chaos come swarming right out of me.

People say that I'm blinded, I say I see.
People tell me I'm in bondage, but I say I'm free.

Everywhere I go, there are eyes staring right at me.
Get away from me storms a raging chaos!
Why must you only follow me.

I'm empty of life and have no power to fight.
Why do you keep me up all night?
These winds have pushed me so far
when I zoom in to reality I'm over taken with fear.

Because I realized Father GOD You were always near.
I go back in, knowing I have changed and You stay the same.
I realized I'm hurting and You've loved me.
I realized these raging storms of chaos
have drifted me away from my destiny.

So please JESUS come forth!
I have nowhere to hide.
Shield me from these raging storms
that I created deep inside.

*Come unto me, all ye that labour and are heavy laden,
and I will give you rest.*

Matthew 11:28

LET GO

When you are tired, let go.

When you are hurting, let go.

When your miserable, let go.

When your heart is broken, let go.

When your running into the same situation repeatedly, let go.

When you are sick of pleasing the world, let go.

When your life is turned upside down, let go.

When tornados of confusion knock you to your feet, let go.

When you are addicted to the voice of shame, let go.

When you feel there is no reason to hold on to life, let go and then hold on to the Savior.

Call on His name and He shall restore you.

Pray without ceasing.
1 Thessalonians 5:17

If my people, which are called by my name, shall humble themselves, and pray, and seek my face, and turn from their wicked ways; then will I hear from heaven, and will forgive their sin, and will heal their land.
2 Chronicles 7:14

SEPARATIONS BRING PERMEATIONS

I did not understand when You told me to leave Holy Spirit, but I heard these words, "Separations brings permeations."

I did not understand when You said to me PEACE when that person raped me of my soul, and then You said, "Pray and walk away." Then I heard Your sweet soft voice speak to me and say, "Separations brings permeations."

I was so enraged when those so-called leaders talked about me like a dog! In addition, I had to pray, and then as I was on my way to punch them right in their face, You said these words grabbing my hands and putting them away, "Wrong weapons. Now drop to your knees and pray. Separations bring permeations."

When I fell so deep in love with this person and they drifted away, and I so desperately wanted him to stay. Moreover, You whispered within my soul, "Separations brings permeations. Continue to pray also be bold."

When the seed of rebellion rose in my children and they rebelled against me and my authority, I wanted to kill them dead and You said to me, "Repent and turn from your foolish ways, now send them away. Separations brings permeations."

When I got saved but I was still around the same people and You said, "Come out from among the heathens." I didn't understand Holy Spirit, but You reached out Your hand from heaven and softly said, "Follow me, I will lead the way. Separations brings permeations."

As I was looked upon because of my faith in You, as my son laid in the bed with no life DEAD. Then you said, "Separations brings permeations."

When you blessed me with a mother at 28, no understanding JESUS I just knew You are great. Separations brings permeations.

Whenever I would smile and Your people would frown. Because You gave me grace no longer bound, I was safe. They laughed and said, "You're foolish. Get away." I remembered. Separations brings permeations.

Every day dealing with rejection from neglections because of my acceptances to you,

"Leave," was the whisper as You pulled me through and words of encouragement, "Later they will understand you. Separations brings permeations."

2 Corinthians 5:17, *Therefore if any man be in Christ, he is a new creature: old things are passed away; behold, all things are become new.* All I can do now JESUS is completely heartily walk in the new. Separations brings permeations.

And when these things begin to come to pass, then look up, and lift up your heads; for your redemption draweth nigh.

Luke 21:28

STAY FOCUSED

It is not about what you are doing,
or what you are getting out of what is being done.
STAY FOCUSED

Do not look at the mountain and say, "It is TOO HIGH!"
Ask God how far He wants you to climb, and take off.
STAY FOCUSED.

Now since you made it to the top the only way down is to jump, deny the
power of procrastination, then move right into your destination.
STAY FOCUSED.

The giant is not the problem.
You just do not believe you have what it takes
to kick that giant clean out of your face.
STAY FOCUSED.

The more you are come against is evidence
that you are growing while soaring.
STAY FOCUSED.

Be free. Come alive. You have the power.
No more complaining, not in this hour. Christ is the Strong Tower.
STAY FOCUSED.

Wake up thou old sleeper. Your feet have been planted on solid ground.
Playing dead? Stop. Just do what He said.
STAY FOCUSED.

You're used to sleeping through misery.
But this is the day that you shall see, you did not want to let it go.
But you must my child, you have to grow.
STAY FOCUSED.

Do not fear your opponents. Once you stand against the enemy
the only thing he can do is tickle your fancy.
STAY FOCUSED.
Simply spread out your wings

and fly soar with the eagles as death has passed you by.
Smiling and shining you have made it.
You have conquered the lie.
STAY FOCUSED.

Even when it hurts,
you still have to push.
You're giving birth.
STAY FOCUSED.

Pulling down darkness capturing the light,
fight the good fight.
STAY FOCUSED.

Brushing off sins, you are at peace.
You win.
STAY FOCUSED.

Now apply the fruit of the Spirit it is not too late.
STAY FOCUSED.

Open up your ear gates,
understanding who is leading you where you should be headed.
STAY FOCUSED.

Stop sowing discord. The light of God is too bright on you.
STAY FOCUSED.

Look up at the sky all your redemptions draw nigh.
Rejections bring misconceptions,
but this day you have been instructed with Godly lessons.
STAY FOCUSED.

For ye are bought with a price: therefore glorify God in your body, and in your spirit, which are God's.

1 Corinthians 6:20

THE BIGGEST LIE OF SATAN

I want to be pleasing to You JESUS but I feel it is too late.
THE BIGGEST LIE OF SATAN

I want to pray to You Jesus, but last night I messed up.
THE BIGGEST LIE OF SATAN

I want to dance before you Jesus but all these people are around
THE BIGGEST LIE OF SATAN

I need to go to church but my schedule says I have to work
THE BIGGEST LIE OF SATAN

I know I should read and study a little bit more but my body is so weak.
It's fine. I'll just fall to sleep. THE BIGGEST LIE OF SATAN

I know I should not be drinking. It's tormenting my thinking.
But it deceives me in a moment of pleasure for a lifetime of pain. THE
BIGGEST LIE OF SATAN

I feel so good. I'll stop if I could.
THE BIGGEST LIE OF SATAN

I know I should cut this person off. It's always something when I'm
around. However, they have been with me since day one holding it down.
THE BIGGEST LIE SATAN

Jesus does not love me because of what I have become.
THE BIGGEST LIE OF SATAN

Will I ever overcome?
THE BIGGEST LIE OF SATAN

I am sick of forgiving people I have been through way too much.
I will just keep this wall lifted all the way up.
THE BIGGEST LIE OF SATAN

I don't need to exercise I don't need to eat healthy I'm alright.
THE BIGGEST LIE OF SATAN

I do not need anybody I got this myself.
THE BIGGEST LIE OF SATAN

It does not take all that. I am good where I am.
THE BIGGEST LIE OF SATAN

You do not have a title so I do not have to listen to you.
There is no way you know more than I do.
THE BIGGEST LIE OF SATAN

I am not paying tithes or giving offering.
That church isn't getting my money. They are so retarded.
THE BIGGEST LIE OF SATAN

It is impossible for grace to reach me in all this garbage.
THE BIGGEST LIE OF SATAN

I know I should save myself for marriage.
But I need to be pleased so let me give in.
THE BIGGEST LIE OF SATAN

I am going to use my title to cause a rival. I am in control.
THE BIGGEST LIE OF SATAN

I do not have to go to church and I do not need a leader.
I am safe right at home doing what I used to do
THE BIGGEST LIE OF SATAN

My life is a playground.
One minute I am excited the next I am down.
You said that I am an overcomer and You whisper, "Come as you are."
I lay all of the burdens down and this day I choose to follow You.
No more shall I be addicted to the biggest lies of Satan.
Amen, it is so.

My sheep hear My voice, and I know them, and they follow Me;
John 10:27 NASB

THE BREATH OF MISERY

The breath of misery keeps you in bondage; especially when should pray.
As it breathes it causing you to be stuck so you can't look up.

Re-evaluate. Whose presence have you been in lately?
The breath of misery tells you to sin and you shall win.

Re-evaluate. Whose presence have you been in lately?
The breath of misery tells you this storm will never pass you bye

Re-evaluate. Whose presence have you been in lately?
The breath of misery causes you to fear, so your death can't hear.

Re-evaluate. Whose presence have you been in lately?
The breath of misery shuts down life and gives you strife.

Re-evaluate. Whose presence have you been in lately?
The breath of misery causing you to bite, stir up confusion, and fight.

Re-evaluate. Whose presence have you been in lately?
The breath of misery pulls you away from the throne.

Re-evaluate. Whose presence have you been in lately?
The breath of misery drifts you so far away, until you're gone like the prodigal son who did not follow or honor his father.

Re-evaluate. Whose presence have you been in lately?
The breath of misery calls you to be so un-submissive to the things of the spirit realm now you're overwhelmed jammed.

Re-evaluate. Whose presence have you been in lately?
The breath of misery tells you to put on flesh
when Christ said let go, take it away.

Re-evaluate. Whose presence have you been in lately?
It is time to let go and chose you this day whom you shall serve.

18 And I say also unto thee, That thou art Peter, and upon this rock I will build my church; and the gates of hell shall not prevail against it.

19 And I will give unto thee the keys of the kingdom of heaven: and whatsoever thou shalt bind on earth shall be bound in heaven: and whatsoever thou shalt loose on earth shall be loosed in heaven.
Matthew 16:18-19

THE RIVERS OF PAIN

As I prepare to face the biggest fears, the rivers of pain call my name
whispering, "Why change?"

As I try to stand and grab your hand, the forces of darkness captures me
from the rivers of pain. Instead of calling Christ, I have chosen shame.

As I try not to cry wondering why this mist of misery will not pass me by,
then I finally realize I am drowning in the rivers of pain

As I try to cope with this brokenness trying to find completeness,
the rivers of pain pull me deeper down.

As I grasp for air I see the threshing winds of "I do not care"
tossing me everywhere.

As I'm drowning sinking deeper I hear a voice telling me I'm a keeper,
I start to see a light.

So, I reach up my hands and begin to speak, oh rivers of pain you have no
power over me I have gained the strength to swim to the shore,
so I give it all I got non-stop.

There is a fight in me. I keep pushing till I reach the top,
I swim and I swim till I'm out.

I can see where I am going and what's my purpose it's to get to the surface
to the land where I shall stand. I represent the GREAT I AM,
the rivers of pain will not capture me I AM FREE.

And he laid it upon my mouth, and said, Lo, this hath touched thy lips; and thine iniquity is taken away, and thy sin purged.

Isaiah 6:7

PURGED

I have to make it to heaven. I have to change my ways.

I have to know without doubting Jesus loves me.

I have to rebuke failure and denounce damage while trusting in the Savior.

I have to prepare for purpose while submitting to righteousness.

I have to never again allow my soul to slip into another spiritual comma.

I have let go of the entire trauma confessing what I am guilty of and testifying about what I have gone through.

I have to not seek the approval of man. I have to take God out of the box.

I have suffered for you King of Glory. I have to crucify the flesh.

I have to worship. I have to learn from You.

I have to take full responsibilities of the wrong decisions I have made.

I have to declare and decree I am redeemed.

I have to be blessed and not stressed.

I have sup with the King. I have to hear Your voice.

I cannot allow self-pity to hinder my personal relationship.

I have to believe that all things, trials and tribulations, are working for my good.

I have to study His Word. I have to stay Kingdom focused and Christ devoted knowing that I have been purged.

For whosoever shall call upon the name of the Lord shall be saved.
Romans 10:13

LORD HELP ME

Lord help me with these negative thoughts.
Lord help me to be positive.
Lord help me not to despise my children.

Lord help me, I am bitter and a quitter.
Lord help me to trust you.
Lord I need you now.

I am stuck in all this abandonment.
Lord help me to think more like you.
Lord help me to see that Jesus made me free.
Lord help me and break off all shackles.

Lord help me not to act as if I am okay.
Lord Help me to cry to you.
Lord help me to have power thoughts.
Lord help me to listen to you.

Lord help me to focus on Your kingdom.
Lord help me to not be lazy.
Lord help me to die to myself.
Lord help me to recognize your glory.

Lord help me to forgive.
Lord help me to make myself available to you.
Lord help me to draw nigh to you.
Lord teach me to really love you.

Lord teach me to be gentle, kind and sweet.
Lord wake me up under your anointing.
You said that those who call to You, You will save and make free.
So Lord come please, I admit I need You.
I am dropping everything to follow you.

⁶ Be careful for nothing; but in every thing by prayer and supplication with thanksgiving let your requests be made known unto God.

And the peace of God, which passeth all understanding, shall keep your hearts and minds through Christ Jesus.
Philippians 4:6-7

THE HURRICANE SYNDROME

I must admit this pain hurts so badly even when I have the urge to pray.
When I get mad it feels as if I am erupting, bursting with winds of sins.
But then again I realize it is the hurricane syndrome.

A year of polluted air causing me to feel as if I just don't care.
I'm not aware. It's so hard to think what they did to me I wouldn't dare.
Hurricane syndrome.

I have been taken by surprise shattered like glass and broken like sticks. It is so heavy. Just like bricks.
Hurricane syndrome.

I am so unstable, unable to pray. Matter fact I chose not to!
But then again I have to.
Hurricane syndrome.

How do I get to you?
Now it is raining and I'm complaining but not maintaining.
Hurricane syndrome.

The pain that I have gone through,
how could I say Father I need You?
Hurricane syndrome.

Belittled as a child even until now.
I frown because I cannot smile.
Hurricane syndrome.

The rocks are falling from this hurricane.
Bursting my mind, I'm out of time.
Hurricane syndrome.

I do not have any might.
So why fight?
Hurricane syndrome.

I got it! I will just fuss and cuss.

That will get things right.
Hurricane syndrome.

Up all night crying, weeping, and peeking
because I know I should follow His way.
Hurricane syndrome.

Please empty me from this disaster.
I've made up my mind. You are the Master.

I put my life down.
You hold the crown.

No more. No more.
Lift me from this floor.

This hurricane syndrome, take it.
I want no more.

Beloved, I wish above all things that thou mayest prosper and be in health, even as thy soul prospereth.

3John 1:2

THE SHACKELS THAT PULL ME DOWN

The closer I get to You
I fall back into this same old cycle of delusion
that causes confusion.

The more my desire is to please You
the more the voices of my past capture me
then the shackles pull me down.

I want what You want for me.
But how is it possible? When these shackles pull me.

These shackles yell and scream.
They hate me, because I am nothing but a disgrace. This is what they say.

They laugh and pull me deeper to the ground.
Saying, "Ha where is your God? He has no crown."

I am so tired of this. I want so much more.
But these whispers of deceptions tell me Father,
that You have closed the door.
So now I am totally in a disaster, confused about my master,
because these shackles slow me down I cannot go any faster.

I hope and pray that this will just go away.
Simply because I need my Savior to show me the way.
I can hear You say, "Come to me. I have made you free."
Then why are these shackles pulling on me?

You begin to show me my past when I was always last,
how the spirit of rejection gave me false revelations
that changed my communications – toward You.

That is why these shackles pull me down.
The more You show me the harder I cry,
bursting with tears of thunder wondering why. How did I let this go by?
I look to You and in these words after repentance,
it is time to let go of my hindrance.

*Now faith is the substance of things hoped for,
the evidence of things not seen.*

Hebrews 11:1

RELEASE

Humility releases stability
that gives Christ the ability,
over obstacles trials and tribulations.

No matter what you face
or how broken you may be,
soon or later you must release.

The great I AM says He is speaking.
But are you listening?
You have to release.

You are such a precious jewel.
But you carry broken treasures.
You have to release.

All that bottled up pain
shows directly on your face.
You have to release.

You're barely smiling
because the pain is so deep.
You have to release.

Why?
Because faith is the substance that is, complete.
Release.

*For verily I say unto you,
That whosoever shall say unto this mountain,
Be thou removed, and be thou cast into the sea;
and shall not doubt in his heart,
but shall believe that those things which he saith shall come to pass;
he shall have whatsoever he saith.*

Mark 11:23

MOUNTAINS

Just push pass the distress
reach forth and grab your deliverance,

stand and rise in the power of his might.
Those mountains are there to train you;

I know it is hard to believe because of what you see.
However, the greater one lives on the inside.

You do not have to be afraid of the size
because they are so big and high;

just call forth the kingdom of God
he will mount you up

You have the power to move those mountains.
You have the authority to make them shrink.
You have the power simply just to speak.

Tilt your head and open your mouth
saying it boldly with force
as His words come out.

No more will you intimidate me
You high mountain this day I cast you out.
I direct you to the seas.

And you shall never get out.
I am victorious! I did it and now it is done.
I'm no longer scared, because the victory is won.

Rejoicing in hope; patient in tribulation; continuing instant in prayer;
Romans 12:12

JUST LET GO

If God took it on the cross,
why are you still carrying it?

Don't get offended.
Just comprehended it.

CHRIST THE MESSIAH has highly recommended
that you just let go.

There aren't any barriers
that He can't delete.

So don't continue to let your mind sink.

Just let go.

PERSONAL REFLECTIONS

Handsome Kings and Beautiful Queens of the Most High KING, have you surrendered the things that keep you from being Kingdom focused and Christ devoted? Even as the raw pain of chaos tries to restrain you, use the following pages to write down the things from which you want our KING to unchain you.

_____
_____
_____
_____
_____
_____
_____
_____
_____
_____
_____
_____
_____
_____
_____
_____
_____
_____
_____
_____
_____

ENDURING

INTRODUCTION

Trying to cope with the pains of my past would sometimes hinder me, until I learned how to endure. I had to completely depend on GOD'S leading and love for my life. Each moment required me to trust in the King, at a deeper level than before. Often I would want to give up and curse the ones who had abused, molested, or caused the most damage throughout my life. Enduring taught me if I did that, it would not solve anything, but it would open more wounds in my life. Because we battle not against flesh in blood, I had to endure while the Holy Spirit cured. Often my attitudes toward the people the enemy used to destroy my identity, were quite harsh. This was so devastating to me, because I could not repay them for what they had done. VENGENCE IS THE LORD'S. I had to forgive and love them in those moments. I had to kneel to the KING and allow Him to bring forth reconciliation that brought freedom not only for me but for them as well.

Enduring allows you to move through the pain while gaining PURPOSE. Hold tight. I can clearly remember the moment I told Jesus that I could hold on. I believed that what I did would make me free. The enemy said I would not. Holding on to those lies, I married a person who battled with mental illness and was also broken just as I was, but did not want to acknowledge the GREAT I AM.

As my mind was being totally restored, I would cry and pray on my knees numerous times, over the fact that my ex-husband would verbally abuse me, and tell me he loved the devil. No matter what I tried to do, the enemy would use him to tempt me to turn back. Thank God it was not so. I would often fast, worship, and pray during the hours my children would attend school.

One particular day, I was crying and yelling at GOD asking Him, "If I am free, why am I still hearing voices? Why is my husband verbally abusing me? In addition, why does the pain from my past still stay so heavy on my mind?" With tears rolling down my face, the Holy Spirit begin to comfort me in a most compassionate way. His presence sat me down on my bed. With His soft calming voice, He said, "Turn on the TV." As I did what He said, Joseph Prince was explaining how grace, mercy, and unmerited favor works. I couldn't believe it because I had been holding on to the fact, that I would never make it to heaven because of everything I had done and what was done to me. What Joseph Prince said was, "THERE IS NOTHING THAT YOU HAVE DONE IN THE PAST OR EVEN NOW, THAT WOULD CHANGE CHRIST'S LOVE FOR YOU." In anger, I said, "Why I am still fearful? The fear is tormenting my mind, and I am tired. I want to be free." The Holy Spirit comforted me again and said, "Listen." As I listened again to the man of god, Joseph Prince went on to say, "THE ENEMY IS THE ACUSER OF THE BRETHREN, HE COMES TO BRING UP YOUR PAST." He went on to quote the precious scriptures James 4:6-10 from Joyce Meyer's Amplified version of the Bible, which reads,

> But He gives us more and more grace [through the power of the Holy Spirit to defy sin and live an obedient life that reflects both our faith and our gratitude for our salvation]. Therefore, it says, "GOD IS OPPOSED TO THE PROUD *and* HAUGHTY, BUT[continually] GIVES [the gift of] GRACE TO THE HUMBLE [who turn away from self-righteousness]." [7] So submit to [the authority of] God. Resist the devil [stand firm against him] and he will flee from you. [8] Come close to God [with a contrite heart] and He will come close to you. Wash your hands, you sinners; and purify your [unfaithful] hearts, you double-minded [people]. [9] Be miserable and grieve and weep [over your sin]. Let your [foolish] laughter be turned to mourning and your [reckless] joy to gloom. [10] Humble yourselves [with an attitude of repentance and insignificance] in the presence of the Lord, and He will exalt you [He will lift you up, He will give you purpose].

In those moments I humbled and repented because of my actions of yelling and approaching the KING in such a manner. Even in the midst of beauty I allowed the enemy to bring fear, no sooner that I repented he came and said, "You are not loved and no matter how many times you cry and pray, I still own you." However, peace quickened my understanding; the Holy Spirit gave me exactly what to say. I opened my mouth and said what the Holy Spirit had told me, "JESUS I believe You love me. But I don't know yet how to receive it. But if You show me how not only to receive Your precious great love, but also how to love You, I will."

Once the prayer of faith went forth from my mouth the power of GOD filled my house and placed me right on my knees in my bedroom. I had never felt anything like this before so I jumped on my bed, and that's when I saw a hand come through the ceiling and touch my face. I knew in that moment I had encountered the KING. All fear had left and no longer did I feel tormented. I was afraid to look up however, because I knew that JESUS was right before my face. He spoke and said, "Do not be afraid. Come closer Lakita. Ask of me anything and I will give unto thee." Although I was shaking and trembling, I knew I was safe. It wasn't the fear like I had experienced before, that had me in bondage. This was reverencing Him and I felt whole. The KING said, "Just let Me love you and when I reveal to you those things that give the enemy the power to control you, do not deny it. Just allow the healing to take place. Repent of it and ask for my forgiveness." I said, "Okay." I felt freedom like I never had as a child. But I felt childlike and joy began to rise up in me.

When I got up I noticed hours had passed. I couldn't believe it! I remember it was around 8 am when I went into my room, because my children had to get on the bus before 8. The time was now 2:00 pm. I still felt burdens and this burden was now my husband. I prayed again and I said Lord, "Why is my husband so cruel to me and my children? You told me he was my husband and that I would be happy and in love." The answer I received terrified my soul. He spoke with grief and said, "My Queen whom I love beyond measures, I never told you to marry him the enemy did. You were in so much bondage that you did anything to please your flesh." JESUS went on to say, "But if you allow me to teach you all things I will give you the endurance to persevere because your destiny is near." I let out a sound that I never heard with tears rolling down my face. "This is too much I do not think I can handle anymore," I said. I went on and asked, "Are telling me I married the devil?" The GREAT I AM said, "You married before your time and you married a devil worshiper." Tears streaming down my face I said, "Teach me what to do. Show me how to trust in You and how to get through this marriage that is full of deception." I saw His hand touch my face as He gently said, "This is the beginning of a miraculous journey with the KING OF MAJESTY." He smiled and said, "Endure the shame while I cure the pain."

From that moment on I had to endure all the lies, abuse, rapes, misery, and pain from my husband. The Holy Spirit gave me the strength to worship, pray, and fast, I had to go to church twice a week while continuously staying in the presence of GOD without ceasing. Each day while my children went off to school and my now ex-husband went to work; I would go drop to my knees and pray. After being done praying, I would just lay at His feet staying in His presence as I confessed of every hindrance. The Holy Spirit would lead me to clean up my home and prepare dinner, even in those moments of freedom I still had to endure the fact that my husband at the time was a devil worshiper. The enemy would use him to text me long messages while I was preparing the home for the family, saying things like my friends just rolled pass and saw you let someone in the house. He would curse me and call me all sorts of names. I would become enraged and immediately want a divorce but the Holy Spirit would say in a peaceful voice, "Endure." There were times when my children and I would be standing by the door being happy of his return. However, he would just come in with the lies of the enemy, saying, "You are just trying to cover up the fact you had those men in this house." He would not acknowledge any of us, only his child that we had together, and would go upstairs to the bedroom.

In those moments, I would have to just smile and continue to be the mother GOD called me to be for my children, I had to endure. Eventually, I would just take his dinner upstairs as I continued to be the wife GOD wanted me to be. My ex-husband would look at me with such an evil look and say, "Come lay with me." My stomach would turn because of the fact he would not ever apologize he would just blame all our problems on me. When we were in bed together, all I could do was pray and ask GOD to take away the disgust so that I could be pleasing unto my husband. His presence would embarrass me and before I knew it, it was over. I had to endure. I learned how to become a submissive wife to someone GOD did not tell me to marry.

Have you made decisions that you believed God told you to make, but you were deceived by your own flesh? Have you come to realize that you believed the enemy? Are you angry with God about your circumstances? Or do you realize that you are suffering the consequences of your own choices? Are you trusting God as you go through? Are you doing all you can to endure? I pray that these poems help you to endure as our KING delivers you from the snare of the enemy.

³⁸ For I am persuaded, that neither death, nor life, nor angels, nor principalities, nor powers, nor things present, nor things to come,

³⁹ Nor height, nor depth, nor any other creature, shall be able to separate us from the love of God, which is in Christ Jesus our Lord.

Romans 8:38-39

POWER

Grace is the favor and the ability to do what I cannot do.
So I declare your POWER to remove all of my failures.

Just the other day I almost slip right back into the pound of bondage
because the hit was too hard but I was able to depend on your POWER.

Without your POWER, Great I Am,
I'm left in religion depending on blurry visions.
Once I tap into your POWER all my needs are met.

This lust in me takes full control
when I decide to please my own dark secrets,
but as soon as I apply your POWER demons flee.

My loins are girded with truth as I face the gates of hell
with your POWER they won't prevail.

No matter what I see I must endure and believe.
It hurts so badly but I have to move forward.
No turning back because of your POWER I can do just that.

³ Thou therefore endure hardness, as a good soldier of Jesus Christ.

⁴ No man that warreth entangleth himself with the affairs of this life; that he may please him who hath chosen him to be a soldier.

2 Timothy 2:3-4

PERSEVERE YOUR DESTINY IS NEAR

The doctors told me I was insane and will always complain,
but I called His name. PERSEVERE YOUR DESTINY IS NEAR

Everything I had was taken away; I was left empty with nothing
but hope so I decided to PERSEVERE MY DESTINY IS NEAR

When I was beaten, spit on, and raped all I could do was
PERSEVERE MY DESTINY IS NEAR

When I could not read, write, or comprehend
all I do was just trust You and PERSEVERE MY DESTINY IS NEAR

When everyone around me turned their backs on me
because of their opinions of me sowing discord and abandonment, the only
thing to do was forgive and
PERSEVERE MY DESTINY IS NEAR

When so-called friends and family members would gossip
and try to hinder my walk with God after the tears
PERSEVERE MY DESTINY IS NEAR

After all the times I was there for you and sought you through,
when I needed you after me and my children were evicted
you did not even come to see about us. I had to
PERSEVERE MY DESTINY IS NEAR

Left with no money for a year but my sweet God made a way
I kept on moving towards the mark
PERSERVE YOUR DESTINY IS NEAR

As I struggled with no transportation for 3 years
PERSEVERE YOUR DESTINY IS NEAR

I leave you with this Queen and Kings of the Most High KING
despite difficulties, failures or oppositions stay in the race PERSEVERE
YOUR DESTINY IS NEAR

Howbeit when he, the Spirit of truth, is come, he will guide you into all truth: for he shall not speak of himself; but whatsoever he shall hear, that shall he speak: and he will shew you things to come.
John 16:13

THE HELMET

The devil knows we are more likely to believe his lies,
if we acknowledge the thoughts as our own.

As we speak from the doubting syndrome
we become more numb to Satan devices.

The helmet of Christ blocks us from strife
while fighting off evil and everything that tries to rule our life.

The helmet protects from thoughts of neglect,
false security, bestiality and cruelty.

The helmet allows me to zoom in on my opponents
while they are plotting against me.

The helmet reminds always, that I am free.
The helmet supplies me with full insurance and coverage.

The helmet assures me of my divine destiny.
The helmet provides me with comfort
when the tornados of un-forgiveness start to move in.

The helmet gives me more strength at my weakest points.
The helmet keeps me at perfect peace even when death confronts me.

The helmet keeps me submitted to authority. When I am on the battlefield
I'm reminded that no weapons formed against me shall prosper.

The helmet reveals to me the times and hours.
The helmet shields me from compromising.

The helmet keeps me in the presence of God.
The helmet gives instructions on how to trust my creator beyond measure;
the helmet draws me to the cross.

The helmet teaches me how to worship in spirit and in truth.

The helmet reminds me repeatedly that I am an ambassador for the Lord.
The helmet encourages me to always testify.
The helmet.

If we say that we have no sin, we deceive ourselves, and the truth is not in us.

1John 1:8

AS I AM

I can remember as a child being abused mentally and physically. I grew up in a very, very dysfunctional house where darkness abided. I was very alone no one to hold me. Every morning I awakened, I could feel the fingers from uncle and cousin, crawling up my legs my little body hopeless, dead.

4-years-old, a broken shattered soul, given empty words of comfort trying to console. Special messengers of Satan, sent to steal my identity, with no voice to tell. Manipulated that if I did I wouldn't live.

But I had already died the moment his hands went places that no grown man should be found, pinning a little girl down. I became afraid of the dark whispers of hatred surrounded my bed, along with the serpent saying, "You might as well give up." Rocking back and forth, screaming until my voice went hoarse, all this hell was driving this child crazy.

How can I live when my life just drifts away? How do I play with my Barbie dolls in an appropriate way? How do I play with my cousins without touching or humping? Trying to tell but hit with the words of rejection. You're just crazy, stupid, bad and lazy. Don't ever mention those word to me again. Now go outside and play, eventually those thoughts will go away.

As I grow older and my heart goes colder, with no protection or shoulder to lean on, the voice of bitterness will not leave me alone. Who would love and take this shattered vase? Matter of fact who would even take me as I am? My soul starts bleeding when the sun goes down. I hear the footsteps of misery coming closer to get me. What do I do? Who can I turn to? Prepare to kill because this pain is so real, at that moment the release from heaven filled the atmosphere and for the very first time I felt safe.

Who are you? Please tell me your name. "I AM the Comforter that heals your shame, renews your strength and changes your name. I have the keys to life, and I love you. Those were not my plans for your life. Give it to me now. There is a process, just do not fall."

His hands went across my face. "But I'm filthy," I said. Remembering His love, I died to rage. No longer was I afraid because I embraced the love from above. He expects me AS I AM.

And he said, Certainly I will be with thee; and this shall be a token unto thee, that I have sent thee: When thou hast brought forth the people out of Egypt, ye shall serve God upon this mountain.

Exodus 3:12

THE RED SEA

For God, the King of Majesty has split the Red Sea
and swallowed up your enemies.

So lift up your cross you are no longer lost.
The staff in Moses' hands represented the Savior of the world, (JESUS).

Once you lift Him up everything that pharaoh (the devil) sent out to kill
you, has been drowned in the Red Sea.

Queens and Kings of the Most High KING
you are made righteous from His blood.

Death has been drowned in the Red Sea.
You have the power just trust and proceed.

Remember your misery has drowned in the Red Sea.
The Father sent His Son on your behalf. Why look to the past?

God moved the heavens just for you.
So walk through the Red Sea.

His all-consuming fire came down and used his son.
The ones that chased you thought they won.

Do not even look back.
You don't have time for that.

Just keep walking through the Red Sea.
Now just believe nothing is too high that God cannot see.

He is who He is.
Now keep passing through the Red Sea.

Beware of false prophets, which come to you in sheep's clothing, but inwardly they are ravening wolves.

Matthew 7:15

YOU CANNOT FOOL ME

You cannot fool me.
I have been fooled before, and I must endure.

You cannot lie to me I am quite aware who the liar is.
I'm moving forward.

You cannot not deceive me I've conquered deception!
I refuse to be bound by false lessons.

You cannot make me believe you're saved.
I have played that wicked game.
It is obvious you're married to shame.

You cannot fill me with vanity
slowly stealing my sanity. I'm free!

You cannot not fool me as if you are a king.
your philosophies are far from Christ's extravagant generosity.

⁵ My soul, wait thou only upon God;
   for my expectation is from him.

⁶ He only is my rock and my salvation:
he is my defence; I shall not be moved.

⁷ In God is my salvation and my glory:
the rock of my strength, and my refuge, is in God.
                                              Psalm 62:5-7

90 DAYS IN A DISASTER

I would not let Him guide me out.
I became bitter, enraged until I began to shout.
I began to doubt.

I knew He was the way
but I became comfortable with a lie.
I did not want to get out.

I felt His presence, but rejected Him.
I did not want to walk down the narrow road.
I became selfish.

My soul, my soul became so fragile,
drifting into every wind,
and most darkened sins.

Oh, Lord! I denied You in a most despicable way.
My 90 days of disaster came
when I denied the Master.

I would not praise You in my storm,
walking around throwing fits,
as I dug myself into a deeper ditch.

I was too proud to beg and to admit,
that I fell out of covenant with the King of Glory.

But I found out that if I do not cry out,
I would die in this disaster.

God I choose to repent and turn away from my wicked ways,
these 90 days felt like a lifetime and I lost my mind.

But I need you to come pave the way.
90 days in a disaster when I failed to trust the Master.

[1] If ye then be risen with Christ, seek those things which are above, where Christ sitteth on the right hand of God.

[2] Set your affection on things above, not on things on the earth.

[3] For ye are dead, and your life is hid with Christ in God.
Colossians 3:1-3

COLLISION

Stop allowing your mind to be crushed,
when your adversaries have been dethroned.

Your emotions have hindered your deliverance.
You are not built to hold trash. You are birthed from purity.

In order to unlock the chambers of restoration have faith.
Block out collisions.

Your soul is locked but your spirit has been freely given.
You know the Word, but you're afraid to apply it.
No more collision. Your help has paved the way.

*[14] I press toward the goal for the prize
of the upward call of God in Christ Jesus.*

[15] Therefore let us, as many as are mature, have this mind; and if in anything you think otherwise, God will reveal even this to you.
Philippians 3:14-15

ACCOMPLISHMENTS

Never give in to what you feel,
go beyond the natural circumstances, dig deeper.

Always be willing to change, never hold on to the pass.
Stay focus on the ultimate prize.

Hope beyond your dreams.
Trust in Christ He is the ruler of your life.

You're moving with the force of greatness.
Your time doesn't matter to God.

Christ is not bound by time.
Take it by force.

Opposition comes when you're focused on the mission.
Look to the cross, and stay in His presence.

If God be with you, who can stand against you? No one!
Always and no matter what, trust God, and die to self.

The enemy wants you to agree with his lies, you are being tested.
LET FAITH ARISE YOU ARE VICTORIOUS.

I lay down and slept;
I awoke, for the L<small>ORD</small> *sustained me.*

Psalm 3:5

THE DESTINY THAT CAPTURED ME

The destiny that captured me and now I'm free,
no more living in yesterday's pain.

I can stand now. His grace removed the burdens
and the destiny has captured me.

I thought the there was no way out until, your destiny captured me.
I believe I could not endure these unbearable situations,
then destiny captured me.

When moments of doubt and disbelieve rushed in, destiny captured me.
As the winds of loneliness would try to push me towards sins,
destiny capture me.

Even in the midst of confusion, destiny captured me.
When no one was there, destiny captured me.

When I tried to find my identity in people, destiny captured me.
The moments of sorrow in frustrating thoughts, destiny captured me.

When I am contemplating on giving up in this walk, destiny captured me.
No matter what you have faced or what you're going through,
destiny has captured you.

*²⁴ Now to Him who is able to keep you from stumbling,
And to present you faultless before the presence of His glory
with exceeding joy,*

*²⁵ To God our Savior, Who alone is wise,
Be glory and majesty, dominion and power,
Both now and forever. Amen.*

Jude 1:24-25

THE DEATH OF MISERY

You are equipped with the word.
If God spoke the universe to existence, you have been made in His image,
why are you so bound with death the of misery?

You are created for holiness, power, and dignity
but you're still captivated in misery?

You are able to call those things that are not, as though they were
but you are afraid of the death of misery.

You won't rebuke the voices of terror that pull you from the finish line,
and yet you say you can read my mind.

The death of misery hinders our walk
and makes us feel as if things are supposed to go our way.

The death of misery comes, when I am too haughty to drop
to my knees because this tribulation blocks my communications.

The death of misery makes me so angry and causes me not to come to you,
that death of misery makes me feel so disgusting and tempts me to quit.

In the end, it actually drew me closer I found out from all of this mess
the death of misery does not have to control me.

After all You are able to keep me from falling,
no more stalling. I'm moving in victory.

And which of you by worrying can add one cubit to his stature?
Luke 12:25

WHY?

WHISPERS
That which causes you slowly to pull away from the things of Christ.

WORRYING
A person that is afraid of tomorrow, because of yesterday's pain.
The mind is too weak to seek purpose and destiny.

BITTERNESS
A deep-planted root of neglect that hinder deliverances.

SLUGGISHNESS
Erupted with laziness birthed from speaking and seeking short cuts
to victory and confessions like it doesn't take all that.

DELUSIONS
One that rejects faith and clings to fear.

Why do we listen to some many lies?
Why do we like hurt?

Why do we as people of the Most High King
allow the enemy to beat us down?

Why do we hold back from the one who sits high and low?
Why are we always competing?

Why haven't we allowed the peace of majesty to rise in us?
Jesus has the answer. Transformation has to take place inwardly.

There is power in the name of JESUS,
so change and focus on His domain and endure.

It's a fact you can handle whatever is set before you.

*¹ If then you were raised with Christ,
seek those things which are above, where Christ is,
sitting at the right hand of God.*

² Set your mind on things above, not on things on the earth.

³ For you died, and your life is hidden with Christ in God.

*⁴ When Christ who is our life appears,
then you also will appear with Him in glory.*
Colossians 3:1-4

YOU FORGOT YOUR ASSIGNMENT

We are subject to the cross and bound by faith.
Your identity did not come from the people who hurt you,
but from the One who is the Chief Governor (JESUS)

As He is calling you up to a place of higher expectancy
move with the momentum.

Why try to prove that you are somebody exposing your flesh?
Your outward appearance has nothing to do
with your inward free salvation.

You forgot your assignment.

Just because you accomplish something from your own works today,
what about the foundation and alignment
of the Son Who won on Calvary?

You forgot your assignment.

The works from your own ideas are enmity towards the King.
And your rituals are making you dizzy. You're going around in circles.

You forgot your assignment.

It is He that makes us free.
Come back to the vine and let Him heal your mind.
There is purpose in your pain.

ENDURE

But if the Spirit of Him who raised Jesus from the dead dwells in you, He who raised Christ from the dead will also give life to your mortal bodies through His Spirit who dwells in you.

Romans 8:11

THE SUDDEN SHORE

Wrapped so tightly in a cocoon of be-littleness
and frustrations even when it's time to fly how can I get by?

Remembering how I became immune to misery
while deceptions are gathering.

There are anchors' holding my soul.
I reach up in hopes and bitter cries that I won't sink.

Then sudden shore steals my ability to cling to the life source.
Now my mind is racing as I am anticipating, should I move forward?

The sudden shore is intimating they come unexpectedly.
These sudden shores are used to me.

They come once I make up my mind,
to dive into my divine destiny.

I know You are able to place my feet on solid ground.
Teach me not to be moved by the sudden shore.

Therefore Pilate said to Him, "So You are a king?"
Jesus answered, "You say correctly that I am a king.
For this I have been born, and for this I have come into the world,
to testify to the truth. Everyone who is of the truth hears My voice."
John 18:37 NASB

CAN YOU DISTINGUISH THE TWO? WHO IS REALLY SPEAKING THROUGH YOU?

Can you distinguish the two? Who is speaking through you?
The reason I'm asking, because what you said left me a little bit confused.
When the bible states that Satan is the author of confusion,
that leads me to believe you're operating from a delusion!!!

Can you distinguish the two? Who is speaking through you?
WHEN GOD CLEARLY SAYS, "I search the heart."
But you said, "I am not qualified because I did not dress the part."
Who is speaking through you?

Can you distinguish the two? Who is speaking through you?
When the precious word of GOD says,
"When he ascended on high HE SET THE CAPTIVES FREE."
I believe that applies for you and me SO ANSWER THIS,
why aren't you free? Who is speaking through you?

Can you distinguish the two? Who is speaking through you?
When my God says He is no respecter of persons. So you try to reject me because you feel that I don't meet your qualifications!!! So you pretty much try to abandon me and fill me up with empty words so you can look down on me!!! OH, I SEE.

Can you distinguish the two? Who is speaking through you?
The Word says He is there to stay.
But you got mad and pushed me away
because I didn't look or do things your way!!!

Can you distinguish the two? Who is really speaking through you?
When the BIBLE says he looks high and low guess what?
He wasn't referring to you SO STOP JUDGING!!!!

Can you distinguish the two? Who is really speaking through you?
When the true living WORD clearly says, He came to give us life you stated I'm headed towards a disaster.
NO that only happens when I accepted your master that cunning SNAKE who caused you to believe it's too late.

I'm not under the law. I reside under GRACE.

Can you distinguish the two? Who is speaking through you?
When the glorious word of GOD says we wrestle not against flesh and blood, why are you bickering among the brethren.
Let me answer that for you.
BECAUSE YOUR GOD OF THIS AIR IS MAD
BECAUSE I KNOW I'M FREE!!!!

Whom the Son sets free is free indeed.
You're operating through a spirit of STRIFE
and you're wondering why you're not saving lives.
Because you will not admit I'm a preacher in a mess you've denied the FATHER and the SON. Claiming to be a best.

But your true identity is you're an enemy of the CROSS
screaming I WON but you're really LOST!!!!
I can recognize that voice it's the thief called DECEPTION.
He has captivated you now he is SPEAKING out of you
from REJECTION!!!!

Preaching false lessons claiming to be a blessing
but you are really stressing.
You are not comprehended of the living word.
That is why everything you say falls on concretes its all-absurd.
YOU GOT YOUR NERVES.

Can you distinguish the two? Who is really speaking through you?
I mean Really!!! I can see the enemy watching me through you.
THE EYES ARE THE GATE TO THE SOUL.
STAND UP PEOPLE PICK AND CHOOSE.

Lift your hands all ye people.
You're lost so you want everybody else to pay the cost
because you made Satan your BOSS!!!!
A DIAMOND IN THE ROUGH
IT'S ABOUT TIME YOU LOOK UP!!!

Can you distinguish the two? Who is really speaking through you?
You made philosophies cures by religiosity
that rejected the cross and CHRIST'S generosity.

Now you are bound by chains - sigh!
ARE YOU GOING TO LOOK TO THE SKY?
Or are you going to continue to walk in PRIDE?
Which by the way is the enemy. You're so blind,
You don't even recognize who JESUS was
praying to in the garden of Gethsemane.

Can you distinguish the two? Who is really speaking through you?
You say you believe but that spirit you carry is downright mean!!!!
Disgusting. You are a witch that's headed to a ditch if you don't quit.
WAKE UP CHURCH!!!

I WAS MADE FOR LOVE the bible clearly says
He came to the CROSS so that I can be free.
So why would he look down on me.

Can you distinguish the two? Who is really speaking through you?
You're bold.
No you actually represent the one who once captured my SOUL.
I notice who is speaking through you
because in the world I acted just like you.
I was deceived which caused me to believe I was the one in charge.
PLEASE.

THE ENEMY IS THE ACCUSER THAT EXPLAINS
why you are a SOUL ABUSER.
Who is speaking through you? Can you distinguish the "two"?
Well guess what? THE ALMIGHTY KING HAS CALLED ME
TO EXPOSE THE WICKNESS THAT'S INSIDE OF YOU.

You're bound by choice
because you won't stop listening to the devil's voice!!!!
You have been bound so long we are sending up war cries because it's
time for you to come home.

YOUR RIGHTFUL PLACE IN CHRIST
you keep trying to avoid Him.
BUT HE HAS BEEN THERE ALL A LONG.
Why would you choose to wear your title, but will not carry your cross?

I AM SORRY. I HAVE TO PUT IT THIS WAY.
But you're lost, trapped behind the gates of manipulation.

Christ said who bewitched you UNHOLY COMMUNICATER.
Your heart is shattered saying things that doesn't even matter.
Your words are vanity completely gone blue.
YOU'RE ON A RAMPAGE
that spirit of blasphemy has taking control of you.

YOU WALK AROUND WITH YOUR CHEST UP
but refuse to lift your shield up!!!!
All along, you have deceived yourself.
Believing you were empowered by JESUS.
NO you are infected with Satan.
WAKE UP CHURCH!

¹ I charge thee therefore before God, and the Lord Jesus Christ, who shall judge the quick and the dead at his appearing and his kingdom;

² Preach the word; be instant in season, out of season; reprove, rebuke, exhort with all long suffering and doctrine.
2 Timothy 4:1-2

LONGSUFFERING

You have to be diligent.
Continue in your faith whether you feel it or not.
Stand firm on Gods promises, for life.
LONG SUFFERING

It's not about the shiny rings or the titles, especially titles with no purpose.
It's about the fact that we are able to suffer
and still smile as he shines through us and for us.
We are able to look to the hills allowing the Holy Spirit to teach us
the things we do not understand through
LONG SUFFERING

No matter how hard, no matter how high the giants' maybe
we can stand firm.
LONG SUFFERING

We are created in God's image and operating in His authority,
we will not waver because of
LONG SUFFERING

I am standing strong
and I am equipped for pain because of
LONGSUFFERING

I won't fall this time
because I know he will never leave me.
LONGSUFFERING

No more of living for man's philosophies.
I am leaning on Christ's generosity
and I will not erupt or give up because of
LONGSUFFERING

I will walk through the fiery trials claiming my victory.
I can do all things through Christ who strengthens me because of
LONGSUFFERING

PERSONAL REFLECTIONS

Enduring is so hard sometimes. Do you struggle to endure? Do you blame others for your pain only to realize that some of the time it is you, that has been in your own way? Or maybe you have been harshly criticized by others who claim to know Christ, but bear no fruit from the Holy Spirit. It doesn't matter how it looks or feels. We must never let those things stop us from crying out for help from our KING. Use the following pages to write down the things you've been enduring, and how the Holy Spirit has been helping you.

NEWNESS

INTRODUCTION

For such a long time bondage was a normal thing to me. Because of the trauma that that held me captivated mentally and physically, if there was not a problem I would go searching for one.

As I began to no longer allow the pain of my past to hinder me, I could literally hear and see the chains breaking. This was not an easy task but I was free at last. I had experienced a love like never before. And in that moment, I had to accept what was before me.

      NEWNESS from the power of the Holy Spirit.

Therefore if anyone is in Christ, he is a new creature;
the old things passed away; behold, new things have come.
II Corinthians 5:17 NASB

THE NEW YOU

As Christians, we can become very discouraged.
But in that moment continue to praise God.

Don't give in because of what it looks like.
It's not what it seems.

We are in the midst of blessing so step out and shout praises to
the King of all honor and glory, and step out in faith.
Thanks to Jesus who leads us down the path of a new you.
He guides us and the moment He starts talking don't stop walking,
continue in your faith.

You want to experience the new you so bad
it makes you thirst for the rivers of life. His love changes your life.

The Holy Spirit was given to teach, care, and always be there.
So follow in His way towards the new you;
anything that is given by God has to fulfill you!

Just because that mask looks as if it is you,
it cannot compare to the New you.

Just because you have been hidden in that dark shadow,
His light still shines.

Just because someone's opinions of who you are overrides your true
identity it's still not the new you.

Just because you have put up this wall it has to fall.
Just because of yesterday's mistake, hurt, misery and pain
that does not apply to the fact that, Jesus knows you by name.

Just because you are a fornicator, the Holy Spirit is still a permeater.
Just because you were raped as a child, Jesus still loves your smile.

Just because you have been divorced by man,
the Holy Spirit still holds your hand.

Just because the doctor says you are going to die, God's Word still applies
– YOU SHALL LIVE.

Just because you may have gotten evicted
you're still equipped with purpose.

Just because that crowd goes to the right
then convicts you with strife; remember you have a new life.

So fight for what's right, the beauty of holiness.
Just because people have failed you, His grace keeps you at perfect peace.

Just because she or he is doing their own thing,
you have to say it is not for me, that's their life,
but I'm following the King.

Just because her eye may be blue,
learn how to simply love you.

Just because they looked down and called you names,
spit in your face and delivered you shame,
remember the Spirit of God has changed the game.

Just because their attitude sucks
you have the power to walk away and continue looking up.

Just because you have a soul tie from the lies of deception,
you have the power to turn then learn stop stressing.

Let the Holy Spirit teach you, it is called a lesson.
Just because you were used to this, or used to having that
you still have to accept the fact that you are new

You were made for love. Keep your eyes above and soar like the eagles.
The tears that have fallen from those precious eyes signifies that
YOU ARE A NEW YOU!

That cold heart is no longer blue.
Destiny has awakened right now, this day IN JESUS' GREAT NAME
in you.

*He hath delivered my soul in peace from the battle that was against me:
for there were many with me.*
                                        Psalm 55:18

THE SILENT WHISPER

The silent whisper that is keeping your eye
on what you want instead of what you have.

The silent whisper that is allowing religion to rise,
instead of grace.

The silent whisper that is drawing you to the voice of error
to abide in terror.

The darkness buried within, that is causing you to sin,
but then again you manipulated the truth
because that silent voice will not allow you to face you.

The silent whisper manifested from confusion
now you are contemplating on a delusion.

The silent whisper that is causing you to reverse the pain,
it is too hard to cope with so now you are belligerent.

Your soul is in a whirlwind but your spirit is planted,
ready to give birth.

But that silent whisper will not allow you to see your worth,
so you are crumbling like dirt.

Because of the silent whisper called hurt
it is time to reach to the sky.

The Holy Spirit says dig within and push out.
You are doing too much thinking so now your soul is sinking.

DESTROY THAT SILENT VOICE.

For the L*ORD* *shall be thy confidence,*
and shall keep thy foot from being taken.

Proverbs 3:26

AS THE WIND BLOWS

As the wind blows, mercies captured my soul.

As the wind blows, the midst of beauty birth forth unity.

As the wind blows, my understanding was no longer drifting among the enemy lines.

As the wind blows, I hear my soul capturing the harmonies of grace.

As the wind blows, I was no longer numb, I found that the victory was won.

As the wind blows, a breeze of humility released stability.

As the wind blows, you pull me into the purpose from the True Vine.

As the wind blows, my mind has been transformed, His beauty leads me on.

As the wind blows, it blew me right in that purpose, (predestined) for me.

I can finally breathe. I'm moving forward…

AS THE WIND BLOWS.

And he humbled thee, and suffered thee to hunger, and fed thee with manna, which thou knewest not, neither did thy fathers know; that he might make thee know that man doth not live by bread only, but by every word that proceedeth out of the mouth of the Lord doth man live.
                                                                    Deuteronomy 8:3

NEWNESS AWAITS YOU

As the Lord speaks, it is not just for that moment, but also for the future
that lies ahead.

I was taught by the King you're deceived by the serpent.
It's time out from perping!

Reach to the sky.
Why?

Because, you have been living a lie just to get by,
with unconfessed sins;
when all you have to do is repent.

Newness awaits you.
The Savior has saved the day!

No more turning back.
You're just too precious for that.

So just look up as His presence fills you up,
and release the pain in exchange for His newness.

Rejection, failure, not being able to trust man,
has nothing to do with the almighty hand
that patiently awaits you.

Once you realize that you have changed
but CHRIST stays the same,
I promise you will and cannot remain the same.

Even though it hurts its worth trusting in the voice of truth.
Trials and tribulations bring character.

Go forth newness awaits you.

*The Lord preserveth all them that love him:
but all the wicked will he destroy.*

Psalm 145:20

RELATIONSHIP VS RELIGION

Religion is based off what you do and how it is done.

A Relationship is when you are not at your best,
I love you beyond measures
and will help you do what is hard for you to achieve.

If you just let go and believe
you cannot have a relationship and religion at the same time.

Religion hurts and is not focused on FAITH but just works.

A RELATIONSHIP with GOD through CHRIST
are the WORKS of JESUS
and His accomplishments on CALVARY
that freely bestowed upon us
the unity and the ministry of RECONCILIATION.

Therefore, QUEENS and KINGS of the MOST HIGH KING
recognize that you are worth it and surrender to your PURPOSE.

*¹ I will bless the Lord at all times:
his praise shall continually be in my mouth.*

*² My soul shall make her boast in the Lord:
the humble shall hear thereof, and be glad.*

*³ O magnify the Lord with me,
and let us exalt his name together.*

*⁴ I sought the Lord, and he heard me,
and delivered me from all my fears.*

*⁵ They looked unto him, and were lightened:
and their faces were not ashamed.*

*⁶ This poor man cried, and the Lord heard him,
and saved him out of all his troubles.*

*⁷ The angel of the Lord encampeth round about them
that fear him, and delivereth them.*

*⁸ O taste and see that the Lord is good:
blessed is the man that trusteth in him.*

*⁹ O fear the Lord, ye his saints:
for there is no want to them that fear him.*

*¹⁰ The young lions do lack, and suffer hunger:
but they that seek the Lord shall not want any good thing.*

*¹¹ Come, ye children, hearken unto me:
I will teach you the fear of the Lord.*

Psalms 34:1-11

YOU MAY HAVE FELL BUT HIS LOVE PREVAILS

You have to go through the process to discover your procession.
It's a blessing. Stop stressing.
Reverencing Christ
is the beginning of a new life.
You may have fell
but His love prevails.

No matter how the voices of hell
try to compel you, they won't so excel.
Don't continue to be unpredictable
to the predictable.
You may have fell
but His love prevails.

Stop looking at how the mountains are
and just climb.
You may have fell
but his love prevails.

Stop procrastinating and activate your faith.
It's not too late.
You may have fell
but His love prevails.

Don't ever look at the mountain
and say it's too HIGH.

You may have fell
but His love prevails.

Speak these words;
HOW HIGH UP DO YOU WANT ME TO GO (James 4:8)?

You may have fallen
but His love never fails.

It is not the size of the mountain that is the problem.
It is your lack of faith that He is the mountain mover.

You may have fell
but his love prevails.

Keep pushing towards that mark
and do not stop (Philippians 3:13-14).

You may have fell
but His love prevails.

Now do yourself a favor,
precious soul created to be bold.

KEEP PUSHING!

You have fell
but His love prevails.

BE FAITHFUL.

⁵ While the bridegroom tarried, they all slumbered and slept.

*⁶ And at midnight there was a cry made,
Behold, the bridegroom cometh; go ye out to meet him.*

⁷ Then all those virgins arose, and trimmed their lamps.

*⁸ And the foolish said unto the wise,
Give us of your oil; for our lamps are gone out.*

*⁹ But the wise answered, saying, Not so;
lest there be not enough for us and you:
but go ye rather to them that sell, and buy for yourselves.*

*¹⁰ And while they went to buy, the bridegroom came;
and they that were ready went in with him to the marriage:
and the door was shut.*

¹¹ Afterward came also the other virgins, saying, Lord, Lord, open to us.

¹² But he answered and said, Verily I say unto you, I know you not.
Matthew 25: 5-12

I HAVE A NEW NAME

I have a new name given by You Great Almighty.
Keep me close and in Your presence. I do not want my lamp to go out.

The more I spend time with You, the more I am enlightened.
Thank You Sweet Savior I have a new name.

I do not want to waste any more time acting as if I am blind
knowing you have forever changed my mind.

Everyone else around me is drowning, lingering, and clowning.
I have a new name, so I cannot do the same.

I have to stay kingdom focused and Christ devoted as the Prince comes near.
Even though I might fear I have to endure and also persevere.

I have a new name as destiny is calling me,
I choose to be wise with what You have given me to do.
And when the doors open I shall come in and meet You.

¹ Now Peter and John went up together into the temple at the hour of prayer, being the ninth hour.

² And a certain man lame from his mother's womb was carried, whom they laid daily at the gate of the temple which is called Beautiful, to ask alms of them that entered into the temple;

³ Who seeing Peter and John about to go into the temple asked an alms.

⁴ And Peter, fastening his eyes upon him with John, said, Look on us.

⁵ And he gave heed unto them, expecting to receive something of them.

⁶ Then Peter said, Silver and gold have I none; but such as I have give I thee: In the name of Jesus Christ of Nazareth rise up and walk.

⁷ And he took him by the right hand, and lifted him up: and immediately his feet and ankle bones received strength.

⁸ And he leaping up stood, and walked, and entered with them into the temple, walking, and leaping, and praising God.

⁹ And all the people saw him walking and praising God:

Acts 3:1-9

LOOK UP

I know it can be so hard to trust in the unthinkable
or maybe the impossible. But Christ is available.

Just LOOK UP!
You must Queen and King of the Most High King.

Close your weary eyes to the physical.
The burden is too heavy.

LOOK UP!
Walk by faith then shall you see in the realm of the supernatural,
the eyes of grace where all worries fade away.

LOOK UP!
Yes, you may be used to the pain and carrying this shame
that is leaking from your vein. Call His name.

LOOK UP!
I hear the voices in rage pulling you back because you found change. Keep
pressing. His glory shall reign.

LOOK UP!
I am weakened and my heart stop beating.

LOOK UP!
I have been addicted to doing things the same.
It is hard to change. That does not matter.

LOOK UP!
I understand when jealously, self-pity, and a competitive spirit tries to
hinder your ability to cry and reach out.

LOOK UP!
Even in the midst of rejection that's keeping your soul in dry places
the sky is not the limit.

LOOK UP!
There is no place so low that His presence can't and won't go and won't flow.

LOOK UP!
Your soul is restored.

Just LOOK UP!
Don't draw back.

Simply LOOK UP!

But thou, when thou prayest, enter into thy closet, and when thou hast shut thy door, pray to thy Father which is in secret; and thy Father which seeth in secret shall reward thee openly.

Matthew 6:6

PRESS IN

You have to prepare for the miracle.
Continue reading and praying.

The truth is JESUS CHRIST through the power of the Holy Spirit, the Almighty Prince of Peace our Lord and Savior has given you life.

If you do not have peace and you are left with strife, press in.
Let him take you to that secret place.

You have a destiny. Press in.
You have been consecrated.

You may not want to go, but you must.
It is time to grow.

Your blessing is on the other side of the wilderness. Press in.
No more eating off the platter of deception from the devil's lies.

If God said it, then it's so. Press in.
And you will know that secrets can't abide where there is Grace.

Press in.
Your old memories have just been erased.

Praying always with all prayer and supplication in the Spirit, and watching thereunto with all perseverance and supplication for all saints;
Ephesians 6:18

CLEAN HOUSE

The devil will not leave because you have not put him out.
Clean house.

Command him to leave. He is cluttering your space.
Clean house.

He can no longer create infestations.
There are critters running rampant.
He tells you it's not happening.
Clean house.

He tells you do not be watchful or pray.
It is really time to clean house.

You barely can breathe because it's just not clean.
Remove the garbage from within your house.

You weren't created for torment, selfishness, or pain.
So clean house.

Evict him. He has to get out. You're created to be fulfilled.
Stay focused. His power is real.

DECLARE YOUR VICTORY!
Now shout!

I SHALL IN THE NAME OF JESUS CLEAN THIS HOUSE!

*If ye abide in me, and my words abide in you,
ye shall ask what ye will, and it shall be done unto you.*
John 15:7

*Thou wilt keep him in perfect peace,
whose mind is stayed on thee: because he trusteth in thee.*
Isaiah 26:3

*For whom the Lord loveth he chasteneth,
and scourgeth every son whom he receiveth.*
Hebrews 12:6

TAKE UP THY BED IN WALK

You're DEAF because you want HEAR.

You're BLIND because you chose not to SEE.

You're STIFF because you won't soften your HEART.

You're paralyzed because you won't TAKE UP THY BED AND WALK.

Change. Don't look at the PROBLEM.
Stay focused on the PROMISE.

The HEAVENS celebrate you.
The angels are FIGHTING for you.

Why sit there and wait?
It may be too LATE.

The rivers are stirring. The currents are moving.
TAKE UP THY BED AND WALK.

*And all things, whatsoever ye shall ask in prayer, believing,
ye shall receive.*
Matthew 21:22

OUR GOD

Our God is a God of love,
and not hate.

Our God is a God of compassion,
and not confusion.

Our God is God of peace,
and not chaos.

Our God is a God of restorations,
not holding any good thing.

Our God is a God of unity,
not discord.

Our God is humble, meek, and kind,
not prideful, ignorant, or enraged at you.

Our God speaks gentle with expressing a heart,
not unwholesome conversing.

Our God is a God of excellence
not good enough.

Our God leads us into all truth with tenderness by His hand,
not judging, condemning, or pointing figures to make a wicked point.

Our God yearns for you to get through.
Just let go of all that hinders you.

Our God is waiting,
just for you.

Then shalt thou call, and the Lord shall answer; thou shalt cry, and he shall say, Here I am. If thou take away from the midst of thee the yoke, the putting forth of the finger, and speaking vanity;

Isaiah 58:9

FOLLOW THE PRINCIPLES AND NOT THE PLEASURE

Pursue the plans and take a stand for wholeness.
Follow the principles and not the pleasure.
It may seem like yeah okay whatever.

But that pleasure that's keeping you in sin
slowly but surely drifts you further in away
from greatness.

It might just be pleasurable.
But what's the purpose after the feeling runs out?
Now you're confused and it seems as if there is no way out.

Follow the principles and not the flesh.
It's havoc.
Don't yield yourself to mess.

I know it's addictive.
But you haven't accepted the calling for your life.
Don't give up yet!

Follow the principles and not the flesh.
Pleasure that goes beyond measure.
No self-control.

When you were bought with a price
He has given you a new life.
But you have to choose the principles over the pleasure.

It's going to get tougher the more you climb.
But guess what? Your connected to the True Vine.
JESUS the Redeemer.

Follow the principles and rebuke the pleasure.
Let Him lead the way.
He cannot fade away.
Refuse IN JESUS NAME

to allow the what ifs,
to keep you from what supposed to be.

Follow the principles and die to the pleasure.
You have been elevated to greatness crowned in royalty.
A citizen of heaven and purged in His beauty.

Be stubborn to failures,
no matter what the situations may seem.
I shall say what thus says the Lord.

Principles and not pleasure.
Even if it looks as if your falling,
CHRIST'S glory is excelling.

Keep climbing,
You're winning even when flesh has lost.
How far are you willing to reach?

Dig deeper you are worth keeping. Principles release purpose.
Make yourself available and live accordingly to the words that He speaks.
For the Holy Spirit is always present.

Keep your faith and you will witness a miracle and blessings.
Act on your faith and do not sit around waiting.
Believe and you shall receive.

Follow the principles and not pleasure.

PERSONAL REFLECTIONS

There is nothing like feeling clean and fresh in your soul! It's amazing how much freer we are to obey our KING when He makes us new. Think about the things that used to be hard to do because you were bound. Use the following pages to write down how differently you think and respond to things now that you know our KING has made you brand new.

RESTORATION

INTRODUCTION

Throughout all of the misery, I was introduced to my purpose. From the entire trauma that occurred in my life, the restoration was the beauty left over from the battle. The Holy Spirit did a spiritual cleansing from the inside out; I was able to live a life full of freedom and newness. There were no more hurts in the late night hours, because I found hope for tomorrow. As the healing over my mind began to flourish, it reminded me of a paralyzed person who could finally walk again. It was refreshing. It seemed like I was in a dream. The enemy could no longer keep me bound with the lies that caused damaged. I saw myself running up hills and even when I fell, the angels would swoop me up. When the enemy would come with false accusations, the healing over my mind would come to my remembrance. I was no longer captivated mentally because restorations had fulfilled me. I AM FREE! HIS GRACE HAS CAPTURED ME. I AM FREE! HE HAS SET THE CAPTIVES FREE. Live forevermore in me KING JESUS. Bless Your Holy name!

As I continued to go through the process of the healing over my mind, the abuse seemed to get worse. I had to face the family members that had sexually abused me. One day at my mother-in-law's, when I went to grab something to eat, I had a very bad feeling in my stomach. I knew by the Holy Spirit that I would have to stand and claim my victory. After my mother-in-law dropped me off which we lived a few houses away from each other, I went into my dining room and began to pray. I cried out and said, "Lord whatever I have to face today don't allow me to face it alone." As His presence filled the dining room, I turned up my radio and the Spirit of GOD led me to K-Love's radio station. With tears streaming down my face I knew I was getting ready to stand against the wiles of the devil. I looked up and at the same time a light shined brightly and the fear of facing a loved one who had sexually abused me ceased. I knew then I had been restored. So I did not have to react to what my emotions were saying, for I was willing to face my abuser with compassion and love.

My cell phone sounded as I received a text message from my male cousin, which was one of the men in my family who had sexually abused me. He asked if it was okay if he could come over to talk about a miracle he received from GOD at work. Now my cousin was very prideful and he battled with homosexuality, he was in denial not only about his lifestyle but also about all the times I would approach him about molesting me. He would cry saying he did not remember molesting me. This was going to be my third time in six years expressing my feeling towards him on how the molestations affected me throughout my life. After the Holy Spirit had given me, peace and instructions on what I should say and what I should not say, peace filled my mind and I was ready to go forth. I responded to the text and told him, "Sure, come over. I would love to hear about your miracle." In the text, he stated he was at my grandmother's house, which was only ten minutes away from where I lived. As I waited, I continued to eat my take-out food. I heard a knock on the door. I did not ask who it was, I just sent my children to their room and I opened the door. In that moment with my cousin I did not know if I should kill him, or let God heal him. My cousin entered my home and as we embraced, I felt him shaking uncontrollably. I begin to pray as we walked into my dining room, I offered him some of my take out and he said, "Yes, I would love some." As I began to share the food I was eating, he started telling me the miracle he received while at work. He started talking about this penny that he had found while cleaning the school. He went on to say how to hear from God and obey, I continued to listen as he went forth; he said that he heard a voice say look down and that's when he said he looked down and saw the penny that he said was worth thousands of dollars. Anger begin to rise because I wanted to talk about what he had done that affected me in my adulthood. The Holy Spirit whispered to me, and said just listen. As my cousin continued talking, he quickly showed me the penny and sat down at the dining room table, the look in his eyes were so wicked. He went on to say that is what you call a miracle. Again my mind began to race as he sat down at my table believing what he experienced was GOD, I allowed the Holy Spirit to give me words to speak.

As we both stared at each other, the great I AM told me to say with a soft and gentle tone, "The miracle was not that you found the penny. It was a miracle that you came through this door and the presence of GOD allowed me to have peace, while inviting you into my home." In that moment I realized that this was not me speaking, because I could never speak in such a gentle tone, for I had always spoken very harshly; especially to those who caused the most hurt. As the Holy Spirit continued to give me words of truth my cousin began to shake, I told him that he can no longer live a life of lies and misery, I continued to speak what GOD was telling me. I told him that I forgive him for all those times he molested me. He looked at me with tears in his eyes and said, "I know you do Kita," and walked out the door. As he left I cried because I knew I was restored and restoration had begun. I was able, through the power of the Holy Spirit, to look my abuser in the face, and tell him I forgive him and I love him and JESUS does too.

Your word is a lamp to my feet
And a light to my path.

Psalm 119:105

THE LAMP STAND

Your past cannot keep you from what's predestined. It's a trap.
Bounce back and use your lamp stand.

Your goal should be to apply His eyes to see.
Strive to reach the heavens and block all distractions,
trusting God beyond measures and through unlimited circumstances,
use your lamp stand.

Stay humble, peaceful, and sweet and don't be move by what you see.
Christ said you're a new creature and He has restored you,
use the lamp stand.

There is a purpose inside of everything
use the lamp stand.

You have come too far to turn off that light.
Stand it's the reason you can see.
Trust in the light and fight the good fight.
It may get tough but continue to look up.

The lamp stand provides you with confidence and hope in your outcome,
be bold and keep the light beaming no more distractions.

I say then, Hath God cast away his people? God forbid. For I also am an Israelite, of the seed of Abraham, of the tribe of Benjamin.
                                                                Romans 11:1

BIRTHING

Do not allow anything negative to come out of your mouth. You have to
stay focus as the glory comes out.

You have been travailing and the gifts are stirring up.
What makes you think that this pregnancy would be easy?

After all the sleepiness and restless nights.
You should expect the unexplainable.

This birth represents restorations, meditations,
and holy communications from the King above.

This baby was birthed through hurt at your lowest point in life. Everyone
one around you would run
and could not stand to be in your presence.

Because that gift inside was so great,
they would often pray that you would miscarry
and have a dysfunctional pregnancy.

The fear of this baby not being accepted by man begin to draw in,
and you almost aborted that awesome seed.

BUT GOD THE KING OF GLORY said, "Not so."
This birthing has to take place.

All worries started to fade away instantly.
The aches of carrying cannot compare
to the fruit that comes with this pregnancy.

That is why your diet was so strict.
It consisted of praise for protein, kindness for water, joy for vegetables,
the word to quench those unhealthy angers, to eat no junk
and praise in place of all caffeinated products.
So be true to the destiny that's in you.

And when I saw him, I fell at his feet as dead. And he laid his right hand upon me, saying unto me, Fear not; I am the first and the last:
Revelation 1:17

THERE IS HEALING IN REVEALING

I have to follow Jesus and let Him lead me.
It's going to be hard but its disciplining me.
THERE IS HEALING IN REVEALING.

The more I spend time with You, Your beauty draws me in.
You're able to show my darkest secrets.
THERE IS HEALING IN REVEALING.

I found out,
I was living for self and not glorifying You.
THERE IS HEALING IN REVEALING.

Now that the Holy Spirit has renewed my strength,
I am able to fly. No more hidden lies.
THERE IS HEALING IN REVEALING.

My past is no longer a threat.
I am redeemed.
THERE IS HEALING IN REVEALING.

No longer do those chains of self-pettiness bind me.
THERE IS HEALING IN REVEALING.
FROM THIS MOMENT ON I CHOOSE TO BELIEVE.

*The Spirit of the Lord is upon me,
because he hath anointed me to preach the gospel to the poor;
he hath sent me to heal the brokenhearted,
to preach deliverance to the captives,
and recovering of sight to the blind,
to set at liberty them that are bruised,*

                   Luke 4:18

FREE

I was blinded and could not see.
I didn't realize how much I needed rescuing,
until He saved me and now, I'M FREE!

I was miserable living a life of deception, battling with hurt and rejection,
not knowing my acceptance until I found thee and now, I'M FREE!

Chasing false dreams polluted with delusions
caused by confusion but now, I'M FREE!

Addicted to sex,
because I had not met You yet but now, I'M FREE!

Denial was my mirror, and terror was my name,
until you came in, Then Your glory reigned and now, I'M FREE!

Torn by depression, heart ripped by neglections,
but Your love mended my heart so now, I'M FREE!

Darkened from the approval of man,
and then You sent Your righteous right hand and now, I'M FREE!

I used to be bound until You found my soul
lingering towards the rivers of pain.
You called my name and now, I'M FREE!

Everything that has been cast down, has been built up.
I no longer have to live by my shattered emotions.
Your grace has found me. Your love restored me and now,
I'M FREE!

*⁹ That if thou shalt confess with thy mouth the Lord Jesus,
and shalt believe in thine heart that God hath raised him from the dead,
thou shalt be saved.*

*¹⁰ For with the heart man believeth unto righteousness;
and with the mouth confession is made unto salvation.*
Romans 10: 9-10

SALVATION

The heavens opened wide above me,
and Christ gives me the ability to move.

I will rest in His presence.
His salvation leads me to my destination.

God I give You all the glory and I thank You Jesus.
You said faith without works is dead.

I have the ability
to come to your throne freely,
because of salvation.

It's time for me to move upon the enemy's line,
and take back what's rightfully mine,
because of salvation.

I know who I am,
and I know where I belong,
because of salvation.

No more am I hidden
behind the wall of rejection,
because of salvation.

No longer do I sell my soul to any man,
but I am married to Thee Man Jesus,
because of salvation.

No longer am I controlled by a competitive spirit.
I can rest with assurance in His identity,
because of salvation.

I am convinced
that my old life has been wiped away, because of salvation.

I am no longer applying myself to drugs,
alcohol, porn, masturbation, and retaliation,
because of salvation.

I no longer debate,
but I can relate to the word of God,
because of salvation.

There is a blessing
in confessing,
because of salvation.

And now I'm resting
and living for Jesus,
because of salvation.

*Not boasting of things without our measure,
that is, of other men's labours; but having hope,
when your faith is increased, that we shall be enlarged by you
according to our rule abundantly,*
                                           2 Corinthians 10:5

CALL IT OUT

Stop battling with the flesh.
Stop convincing yourself that the enemy is not there
when you know that he is, and call him out.

As the gracious Savior
changed and removed my wicked behavior,
I now recognize the Savior.

I am enlightened and I'm not bound.
So teach me Lord
to call the enemy out.

When he uses devices and trickery
to deceive me about my identity help me Savior
to call him out.

When obstacles rise above me,
and it seems as if I'm drowning in misery, help me Lord
to call him out.

When the voice from my flesh tells me,
you are not the best, help me Jesus
to call it out.

When I become death to the voice of truth,
help me Jesus to follow you,
and call it out.

When I know you have opened the door for me to testify
and pride tries to rise help me Jesus
to call it out.

When I am trapped in a blurry vision,
hopeless, nowhere to turn to, help me Jesus
to call on You.

When I am pressured,
when I and tested to give up on You, help me Jesus
to call it out.

When I want to go back to my old ways,
and I know You have saved me, help me Jesus
to call it out.

When I want to cling to foolishness,
help me Jesus
to call it out.

When I want to be fake
and not have faith, help me Jesus
to call it out.

I have to receive
in order to believe even when my enemies start barking
my faith keeps me walking.

Even when I am tossed by the storms,
Your grace leads me on.
Help me Lord to call on You.

Take my yoke upon you, and learn of me;
for I am meek and lowly in heart:
and ye shall find rest unto your souls.

Matthew 11:29

REST IN THE TEST

When you are pressed you are being tested.
Rest simply means it's absolutely complete.

The tests are set up for you to win,
if you believe.

But you have to move from that place of disbelief.
Do not get stuck in that place of distractions.
It holds you captive.

Giants are made to fall. Mountains were built to climb.
Now fall in line. Rest in the test.

Facing trials and tribulations brings hesitation
which is totally unbearable at that moment;
especially when you are hoping for the opposite of what's in front of you.
Rest in the test.

You are soaring toward your future.
Don't get pushed by the winds.
Rest in the test.

Even when everything around you seems empty,
you are full of life, so rest in the test.

It seems impossible and the battle unstoppable
but you are winning and beginning a new life with the King.
So rest in the test.

You may be running a race
but your pace is slow,
but still rest in the test.

There is greatness ahead of you
and your past won't condemn you,
so rest in the test, and receive your inheritance.

*For God hath not given us the spirit of fear;
but of power, and of love, and of a sound mind.*
2 Timothy 1:7

FEAR NOT. COME ALIVE.

Fear has been released through doubt and disbelief,
Faith comes by hearing and hearing by the word of God.
If you are not hearing the word of God.
You will accept fear so you can't persevere.

Fear of the destroyer it is the enemy himself.
Satan in disguise, the contaminator comes to discontinue and purification
of our Righteous King that was bestowed upon you.

Fear is the devil's identity.
He wants you to abide in fear, so that you can be a disgrace
and never understand grace.

Fear not and come alive!
Jesus Christ has set you free.
When fear comes knocking at your door, answer it with faith.
The Blood of Jesus! He has set the captives free.
No more will we accept anything less.

Fear not and come alive!
There is no peace, in the devil's playground.
There is no understanding in his bosom.
There is total chaos and false evidence appearing real.

Fear not and come alive!
You have the power and the authority to tread upon your enemies.

Fear not and come alive! Just because you don't see it yet,
does not mean, it hasn't already happened.

Fear not and come alive!
Just because the devil said that you will die Christ has made you alive.

So fear not and come alive! Don't accept anything less Jesus is the leader
and the hope for tomorrow so rise and come alive.
So rise, fear not and come alive!

*A man's belly shall be satisfied with the fruit of his mouth;
and with the increase of his lips shall he be filled.*
                                                    Proverbs 18:20

DIG DEEPER

Trust in God with your mind.

Dig deeper you are a keeper.

Dig deeper for a divine connection.

Dig deeper for your destiny.

Dig deeper for miraculous healing.

Dig deeper and yearn for a personal relationship.

Dig deeper to overcome self-addictions.

Dig deeper for overcoming.

Dig deeper to speak truth.

Dig deeper to detach yourself from weariness.

Dig deeper to meet God.

Dig deeper to expand your comprehension of our King.

Dig deeper for understanding.

Dig deeper to worship.

Dig deeper to praise, dig deeper.

When you are tired of living in uncomfortable sins cling to the Comforter.

His ways are always refining.

So dig deeper.

*Wherefore he saith, Awake thou that sleepest,
and arise from the dead, and Christ shall give thee light.*
                                                    Ephesians 5:14

WAR

You are a child of God. The enemy hates you beyond extreme.
He wants you under his authority; which is to steal, kill and destroy.
Instead of having authority and his dogmatic lies,
he wants you to feel condemn to death
because it is WAR TIME.

He wants you to follow the rules and regulations of man.
He wants you to be bound and taken as his prisoner.
He does not want you to know you are free,
by grace mercies and unmerited favor.
Nothing you have done as a child or even in your adulthood
can change God's love towards you that abounds
throughout the heavens,
because it is TIME TO WAR.

That thief called deception's job is
to kill hopes, kill joy, kill intelligence, and steal happiness.
It is TIME TO WAR.

It ultimately destroys your humility.
The devil is a liar. Read Psalms 23.
It is TIME TO WAR.

You have to be willing to lose before you gain.
Lose doubt and gain faith.
Lose self-pity and gain confidence in Christ.
Embrace a new life and rebuke strife.
It is TIME TO WAR.

God is preparing us for battle.
Recognize his traps.
It is TIME TO WAR.

Oh let the wickedness of the wicked come to an end; but establish the just: for the righteous God trieth the hearts and reins.
Psalm 7:9

AWAKEN IN YOUR SPIRIT

There is a wolf that's comes in sheep's clothing.
His job is to catch and eat you alive.

You have to stand against the wiles.
Awaken in your spirit, even when it hurts.

Christ's love is still sufficient.
Awaken in your spirit.

If it is tearing you down and not building you up, it is time to look up.
Awaken in your spirit.

If it is draining you of your life source, it is sent to destroy you.
Awaken in your spirit.

You have to live for truth and rebuke the lies. Let restoration come forth.
Awaken in your spirit.

SING UNTO THE BEAUTY OF THE MOST HIGH!

I love suffering, even though it hurts; but it pulls me closer to You.
Gazing upon Your beauty redirects my mind in the midst of temptation.

I am no longer attracted to neglect,
because You have placed my feet on solid ground.

Gazing upon the beauty of the Most High
allows me to reach to the sky with no condemnation.

The enemy taunted me with my past.
I gave him my future but that did not last.

You told me I was a conqueror now my soul is at rest,
I gaze upon the beauty of the Most High.

My frown is now a smile;
You are worth the while.

I am no longer in a shell,
because Your love prevailed.

From Gazing upon the beauty of the Most High,
I can lift my head as I am raised from the dead.

From gazing upon the beauty of the Most High,
Your beauty has captured my mind, restored me, and redeemed the time
from gazing upon Your beauty.

*⁴ Shew me thy ways, O Lord;
teach me thy paths.*

*⁵ Lead me in thy truth, and teach me:
for thou art the God of my salvation;
on thee do I wait all the day.*

Psalm 25:4-5

THE LOVE THAT STOLE MY HEART

I never had a love so precious like this.
I never knew I could love so hard.

Your grace swept me right out of misery that I landed,
right into Your consoling arms.

I never had a love so precious like this,
that when it called my name shame had to lose it bounds.

I never had a love so precious like this.
At the sound of Your voice, the fear of being loved had loosened its grip.

I never had a precious love like this.
Over every obstacle You were my landing point.

Facing every mountain, You were my strength of encouragement;
never had a love so precious like this.

I am not afraid of change.
I am not afraid to look in the mirror.

I am not afraid to confess when I am in a mess.
Because I have never had a love so precious like this.

He that hath an ear, let him hear what the Spirit saith unto the churches; To him that overcometh will I give to eat of the tree of life, which is in the midst of the paradise of God.

Revelation 2:7

OVERCOMING

O   Obstacles may seem to overtake you. Do not give up just yet. Press towards the mark. You are OVERCOMING the odds.

V   Victory is already won and your new life in CHRIST has just begun.

E   Eternity with CHRIST JESUS is where your soul shall finally find rest. The best is yet to come.

R   Refuge, my strength and You are my high tower SWEET JESUS.

C   Certain situations bring manifestation, so let permeations begin.

O   Omni-potent and awesome You are. When everything passes away You will still be THE GREAT I AM.

M   Mindful You are because out of the darkness that I lived for, You still desired to live in me.

I   Integrity is what You have given me and I was able to let go of the misery.

N   Never-ending is Your love. That is why my arms stay lifted to the One above.

G   Grace and mercies saved me and I shall forevermore give You all the praise.

And even to your old age I am he; and even to hoar hairs will I carry you: I have made, and I will bear; even I will carry, and will deliver you.
Isaiah 46:4

NO MORE WHIRLWINDS

I am so tired of being thrown to the ground,
from these dogmatic whirlwinds.

I am so fed up with speaking out of my mouth
that I want to be free then this whirlwind comes and traps me.

I feel so degraded when I finally made it
and then this whirlwind pulls me back to the beginning of the line.

I am so ready to give up because of these whirlwinds;
they just will not give up.

Tossing me here, pulling me there,
and operating in that.

I am just tired of these whirlwinds.
They blow the dust right back on me.
They blow the rejection right back on me.

These whirl winds wrap me up in a spiritual coma
and I am tired of these whirlwinds.

How do I block these whirlwinds from invading my space?
How do I stop these whirlwinds from blowing all this filth in my face?

How do I stop these whirlwinds from plotting against me
so that I can see clearly down the path of righteousness?

I decided to not dwell in that place, where the whirlwinds can form.
I decided to do as You say, so that the whirlwinds cannot blow my way.
I am sticking with Jesus.

I wait for the Lord, my soul doth wait, and in his word do I hope.
Psalm 130: 5

GOD WANTS YOU

You can stop the power of God
through ignorance doubt and disbelief.
God wants you.

You can stop His power to heal you
from activities of the flesh.
God wants you.

You will not grow
from believing in the voices of error and self-rejection.
God wants you.

You do not have time to be blinded by a myth.
Gain strength from the Most High God
and reach to the top where life is unstoppable
and healing is always available.
God wants you.

*A fool uttereth all his mind:
but a wise man keepeth it in till afterwards.*

Proverbs 29:11

SELF-CONTROL

As God tells me what to do,
I shall be true,
for I am renewed walking in my destiny.

I cannot be bound or live in fear.
I have to have control,
because I know He is near.

I will not waste any time
being blinded in my own thoughts,
but I have self-control.

Because it is Him who controls me.
I will not be loose minded
but I will stay Kingdom focused and Christ devoted.

My hope is that control will continue to hold me.
My hope is that His newness will restore me.

Self-control gives me the ability to tread upon my enemies.
So from this moment on,
self-control has the right to freely live in my life.
In Jesus Name.

My sheep hear my voice, and I know them, and they follow me:
John 10:27

OVERSEER

As I lean towards the edge, doing what He says
I cannot see but I trust in the Overseer.

As I speak with the trumpets that blow
I do not understand but I trust in You, the Overseer.

When I was hurt, battered and broken
I still had to be real as the Overseer led me.

Even in the midst of total chaos, You told me to trust in Your eyes,
because they do not sleep.

When family and friends talked about my walk,
Your whispers renewed the strength in my heart the overseer.

I will not be ashamed to call Your name. You see what I cannot see,
You are my hope for tomorrow.

Even when others do not understand You are my eyes,
You are the victory and I will not faint or grow weary
because I trust in the overseer.

Hereby perceive we the love of God, because he laid down his life for us: and we ought to lay down our lives for the brethren.
1 John 3:16

I AM CHANGED

I no longer surround myself with people who will try to hurt me,
I no longer need to feel as if I am suffering from past hurts
I AM CHANGED.

I no longer look for your opinion of me,
for Christ has redeemed me
I AM CHANGED.

I no longer stay up in the late night hours crying for what I did that day.
I sleep peacefully for
I AM CHANGED.

I no longer hide in the dark for I am the light.
I AM CHANGED.

I am no longer in denial.
I AM CHANGED.

I no longer have a taste for death.
I AM CHANGED.

I no longer have to find love in all the wrong places.
I AM CHANGED.

I no longer have to be a part of cliques.
I AM CHANGED.

I learned how to be content for
I AM CHANGED.

I am no longer bound by the what ifs
that keeps me from what is supposed to be.
I AM CHANGED.

I am no longer worried about what they say about me
because I know what He says about me.
I AM CHANGED.

I no longer have to follow the crowd.
I AM CHANGED.

I no longer need recognition from man.
I AM CHANGED.

I no longer keep my head low for
I AM CHANGED.

I found out that I was loved
so it was impossible for me to stay the same.
I AM CHANGED.

Hereby perceive we the love of God, because he laid down his life for us: and we ought to lay down our lives for the brethren.
Hebrews 4:16

WE WON'T BE AFRAID

We won't be afraid of who You are. We shall behold your glory,
so with Your lightening move upon us.

We won't be afraid to present our bodies as a living sacrifice,
holy and acceptable unto You.

We won't be afraid to dance before You.

We won't be afraid to desperately seek Your face.

We won't be afraid to thirst after Your righteousness.

We won't be afraid to drop everything to follow You.

We won't be afraid to humble ourselves before You.

We won't be afraid to allow You to remove and restrict our minds.

We won't be afraid to be connected to the True Living Vine.

We won't be afraid to cry out to You.

We won't be afraid to share Your word the Gospel.

We won't be afraid to be bold and courageous.

We won't be afraid to mount up high as eagles do.

We won't be afraid to sup with You.

We won't be afraid of who You are
for we are created in Your image and You have redeemed the time.
WE WON'T BE AFRAID

But he answered and said, It is written, Man shall not live by bread alone, but by every word that proceedeth out of the mouth of God.

Matthew 4:4

I'M STICKING WITH JESUS

You walked with me. You held my hand.
You let me know that You are more than just a friend.
I'm sticking with Jesus.

You kept me high
when I was low.
I'm sticking with Jesus.

You loved me
when I was unlovable.
I'm sticking with Jesus.

In the midst of temptation,
You gave revelation.
I'm sticking with Jesus.

I had to face the pain so Christ can reign
in those dark areas that I buried.
I'm sticking with Jesus.

In the midst of deception that blocked my blessings,
You taught me a lesson.
I'm sticking with Jesus.

When my heart started beating
You greeted me with purpose.
I'm sticking with Jesus.

When everything around me went dark,
I still saw the light.
I'm sticking with Jesus.

When I did not have any words to speak
You fed me manna.
I'm sticking with Jesus.

I know now that there is nowhere to go,
no mountain too high, no mountain to low.
I made my choice that wherever you go I will follow.
I'm sticking with Jesus.

When all else failed me
Your grace sustained me.
I'm sticking with Jesus.

[14] Ye are the light of the world. A city that is set on an hill cannot be hid.

[15] Neither do men light a candle, and put it under a bushel, but on a candlestick; and it giveth light unto all that are in the house.

[16] Let your light so shine before men, that they may see your good works, and glorify your Father which is in heaven.

Matthew 5:14-16

JESUS IS THE WAY

Break out from insanity.
It is a generational curse that has tried to bury your cross
to make Satan your boss.

Any time an enemy speaks,
they contradict God's word to fit into their liking.
There has been a war cry for you.
Jesus is the way!

Christ is calling you to be the salt of the earth.
But you have not been seasoned. The pain has you screaming.
Stop listening to your enemies.
Jesus is the way!

It is blinding you from your mission
and they are empty words of vanity.
They leave you astray to make Satan your god.
Jesus is the way!

Do not allow unconfessed sins
to pull you into a congregation of death.
Jesus is the way!

When the word is being preached it saturates the atmosphere.
It paves the way for the Spirit of Life to come in,
and then restoration takes place.

Glory Halleluiah! Do not let wickedness defile you.
He hears your soul crying out.
Jesus is the way!

Your inner man has been lifted up.
It recognizes its purpose. No more perping.
Rise, rise and rise.
JESUS IS THE WAY!

Every branch in me that beareth not fruit he taketh away: and every branch that beareth fruit, he purgeth it, that it may bring forth more fruit.
John 15:2

THE VINE

The grapes and bread represents plenty.
God has established a covenant with you and I,
due to your obedience and suffering.

Even when all else complains and all else fades
you remain faithful.

Even when your surroundings did not trust the true living God,
you stood and fought through the process.

Leaning on God and trusting in His timing He moved on your behalf,
you are able to eat and your belly never goes hungry, drinks and never
goes thirsty or lacks any good thing from the True Vine.

Kings and Queens of the Most High King
know that your identities are connected to the Vine.

Cast down anything that hinders your mind.
Block out anything that comes to slow your process,
and rebuke everything that tries to get you to turn from the True Vine.

The True Vine is your life source.
The True Vine's roots run deep in you.

The True Vine heals, restores and uplifts.
The True Vine never forgets who you are.

You have come too far to disconnect from the True Vine.
Move forward.

PERSONAL REFLECTIONS

If we really intend to fulfill our purpose, being connected to Jesus is mandatory. As we Let Go and Endure in the Newness He has prepared for us, Restoration comes quite naturally. Without the chaos and pain that had us bound our lives and relationships can be restored – if we obey the Holy Spirit. Kings and Queens of the Most High King, our KING had a plan when He created us. As you use these final pages to write down areas you long to be restored, it is my prayer that you will be so free in Christ that your purpose in Him will spring forth unhindered, restoring everything Satan stole from you.

_____
_____
_____
_____
_____
_____
_____
_____
_____
_____
_____
_____
_____
_____
_____
_____
_____

ABOUT LAKITA PATTON

Filled with joy over her conversion to life in Jesus Christ, Lakita Patton, shares her testimony of deliverance at every opportunity. Growing up in a family where witchcraft, sexual, physical, and mental abuse was common, Lakita, was the second eldest of eight children. Despite the adult presence of her mother, aunts, uncles and cousins she was left with the full responsibility to take care of three younger siblings. Molested at the tender age of four-years-old by an uncle, she was manipulated by her own grandmother into believing that she was the guilty one. After years of abuse, mental torment began. Dogged by satanic voices which threatened to kill her or force upon her the same fate as her father, who suffered from mental illness, Lakita was unable to escape those in her home that consistently abused her physically and verbally. It's no surprise that the incest and abuse caused Lakita to become very angry, hateful, and promiscuous.

Filled with self-hatred after the loss of her innocence, by the age of fourteen she was pregnant with her first child in a relationship that led to still more physical and mental abuse. Sexual impurity soon became lesbianism and pornography. A stripper at twenty-one years old, Lakita sold her body for money and became an alcoholic. Eventually anxiety and depression led to her diagnosis as a paranoid schizophrenic. As the years of physical, emotional, and mental bondage went by Lakita came close to executing a plan to kill her own children and commit suicide.

It has been four years since that horrific moment. Now clothed with the sound mind provided in Christ, Lakita is free! As she shares her testimonies of God's miraculous deliverance, others are filled with wonder at the power of God's truth and mercy and lives are changed. God has called Lakita to preach deliverance to the captives, to show those who are in bondage and paralyzed in fear to overcome the lies of the devil by renewing your mind in the Word of Jesus Christ. The mother of six children, one of whom is deceased, Lakita currently resides in Pontiac, Michigan.

To contact Mrs. Patton

Mrs. Lakita Patton
c/o PriorityONE Publications
P.O. Box 34722
Detroit, MI 48234

info@LakitaPatton.com
www.LakitaPatton.com

www.ingramcontent.com/pod-product-compliance
Lightning Source LLC
Chambersburg PA
CBHW071615080526
44588CB00010B/1150